George Sand

George Sand

MARTINE REID

Translated with an introduction by
Gretchen van Slyke

The Pennsylvania State University Press
University Park, Pennsylvania

Frontispiece: Nadar, portrait of George Sand, 1864. Photo: Wikimedia Commons (Ministère de la Culture—Médiathèque de l'architecture et du patrimoine—diffusion RMN).

Library of Congress Cataloging-in-Publication Data

Names: Reid, Martine, author. | Van Slyke, Gretchen Jane, translator.
Title: George Sand / Martine Reid ; translated with an introduction by Gretchen van Slyke.
Other titles: George Sand. English
Description: University Park, Pennsylvania : The Pennsylvania State University Press, [2018] | Originally published in French: Paris : Gallimard, 2013. | Includes bibliographical references and index.
Summary: "A biography of the celebrated nineteenth-century author George Sand. Examines her public image, her relationships with her husband, lovers, and children, and her lifelong political commitment"—Provided by publisher.
Identifiers: LCCN 2017060111 | ISBN 9780271081069 (cloth : alk. paper)
Subjects: LCSH: Sand, George, 1804–1876. | Novelists, French— 19th century—Biography.
Classification: LCC PQ2412 .R4513 2018 | DDC 843/.8 [B] —dc23
LC record available at https://lccn.loc.gov/2017060111

Published by The Pennsylvania State University Press, University Park, PA 16802–1003

The Pennsylvania State University Press is a member of the Association of University Presses.

It is the policy of The Pennsylvania State University Press to use acid-free paper. Publications on uncoated stock satisfy the minimum requirements of American National Standard for Information Sciences—Permanence of Paper for Printed Library Material, ANSI Z39.48–1992.

Contents

Foreword

George Sand was no man but quite an exceptional woman. Amantine-Aurore-Lucile Dupin, who would take the name George Sand some thirty years later, was born in 1804 to an aristocratic officer in Napoleon's army and a working-class woman who had made her way to this union in shady ways. When writing her autobiography, Sand would proudly declare that in her veins there commingled the blood of both kings and humble folks. After her father unexpectedly died in 1808, her mother and her paternal grandmother had very different ideas about how Aurore should be reared and fought over the little girl's upbringing. Finally buying off her daughter-in-law, Aurore's grandmother gained custody of the girl and raised her on the country estate at Nohant where Aurore's father had grown up. Aurore spent a good part of her childhood romping with peasant children in nearby fields and woods when she could, receiving lessons from her father's eccentric preceptor, and grudgingly complying with her grandmother's rules for ladylike decorum. When Aurore was twelve or thirteen, she began rebelling against her grandmother's expectations and saying that she wanted to go live with her mother in Paris. Seeing no alternative, her grandmother detailed her suspicions about Aurore's mother's promiscuous past and present. These revelations precipitated a crisis for Aurore. Coming to hate herself as well as her mother, the traumatized girl became quite unmanageable. Aurore was subsequently packed off to the convent of English Augustinian Sisters in Paris, where she spent the next two years dreaming up pranks with other boarders and finally feeling herself called to the religious life. Aurore was not yet sixteen when her elderly and ailing grandmother took her back home to the country. Her grandmother died when Aurore was seventeen, at which point she suddenly found herself the proprietor of Nohant and the vast property surrounding it. Within another year Aurore, now the wife of Baron Casimir Dudevant and soon to be a mother, was following the domestic path that most women of her station and wealth took in early nineteenth-century France.

The marriage was not a happy one. Casimir drank, hunted, and sought the company of women less complicated than his moody wife. Irritated by the suffocating constraints of her life, Aurore took great interest in books as well as in men who read and wrote them. She began writing a bit herself and met Jules Sandeau, a young man who dreamed of a literary career. After heated quarrels with her husband, Aurore in 1831 worked out an arrangement with him so that she could go off to Paris with Jules Sandeau. There they published under the pen name "J. Sand" a few short stories and a novel written mainly by her. Her first big novel, *Indiana*, published in 1832, was signed "G. Sand." By the mid-1830s the literary career of the author henceforth known as George Sand—who would become as famous for wearing men's suits, smoking cigars, and collecting famous lovers, such as Alfred de Musset and Frédéric Chopin, as for her novels and plays—was well under way. An outspoken feminist, socialist, anticlericalist, and idealist, she would continue writing and publishing until her death in 1876. During her lifetime she enjoyed a reputation as one of the great authors of the nineteenth century and earned the praise of writers such as Honoré de Balzac, Gustave Flaubert, Henry James, Ivan Turgenev, and Fyodor Dostoevsky.

This biography takes into account the numerous biographies, in French and English, that have already been devoted to the most famous woman writer in nineteenth-century France. Drawing on these sources, as well as Sand's novels, plays, autobiographical texts, and correspondence, some of which have been published only in the last few years, this biography stands apart from the previous biographies in several notable ways: it gives a central place to literature, without which there would not have been the phenomenon known as George Sand; it closely examines the meaning and importance of the name George Sand (how the choice of this pen name resulted from the particularly complex personal experiences of the budding author, and how this name ultimately came to designate a public image with which she came to identify); it reveals multiple facets of the life of George Sand, not just her husband, lovers, and children or the books and plays that she wrote, but also the various expressions of her political commitment, in addition to her wide-ranging artistic and scientific interests and the ways she organized her days and nights in a busy household. Incorporating texts by and about Sand that have been published only recently, Martine Reid endeavors to draw the most complete portrait possible of George Sand. She also strives to put forth a candid, even-handed, and analytical representation of a remarkable woman in remarkable times. Her overall aim has been to put Sand in the place that she deserves in history, as one of the great authors of nineteenth-century France, standing alongside Victor Hugo, as well as Balzac and Flaubert, who were her friends and correspondents. With its clear, flowing language and impeccable scholarship, this biography will be of great interest to specialists on Sand. At the same time it will sustain the interest of general readers curious to know more about the celebrated and vilified woman who wrote and lived so abundantly.

—GRETCHEN VAN SLYKE

Chronological Points of Reference

1804 1 July: Amantine-Aurore-Lucile Dupin is born in Paris. Her father, Maurice Dupin, is an officer in the army and the son of aristocrats established at Nohant, in Berry. Her mother, Sophie Delaborde, is the daughter of a Parisian bird-seller. The young couple, who have been together for several years, are married on 5 June. Maurice Dupin is already the father of Hippolyte Chatiron, a son whom he did not recognize; Sophie Delaborde already has a daughter from an earlier affair, Caroline Delaborde, and has lost several children in their infancy. Maurice and Sophie have already had two children together, these also dying in infancy.

1808 Sophie Dupin joins her husband in Spain where he is stationed with Napoleon's army.

12 June: Their son, Auguste-Louis, is born in Madrid. In July the family returns to France and takes up residence in Nohant with Maurice's mother, Mme Dupin de Fancueil.

8 September: The infant son suddenly dies.

16 September: Maurice Dupin dies at La Châtre after a fall from a horse.

1809 For financial reasons Sophie Dupin gives up custody of her daughter to her mother-in-law and returns to Paris. Aurore grows up at Nohant and receives a rather curious education under the direction of Jean-François Deschartres who is also in charge of schooling her half brother, Hippolyte. Her mother spends a few weeks at Nohant every summer, and Aurore occasionally visits her in Paris.

1817– Aurore is sent to the convent of English Augustinian Sisters,
1820 rue des Fossés-Saint-Victor in Paris. There she makes friends with several students. Having become very devout, she thinks for a while about taking religious vows.

1821 Mme Dupin dies after a long illness during which her granddaughter does a lot of serious reading at her bedside. Aurore, at age seventeen, inherits the château of Nohant and the vast property surrounding it.

1822 17 September: Aurore Dupin and Casimir Dudevant are married in Paris. He is twenty-seven, the recognized illegitimate son of Baron Dudevant, who lives at the château of Guillery in Lot-et-Garonne. The couple settles at Nohant a few weeks later.

1823 30 June: Maurice, the first child of Aurore and Casimir Dudevant, is born in Paris.

1824 After stays in Nohant and Plessis-Picard, the couple moves to Paris at the end of the year.

1825 They travel to the Pyrenees. There Aurore, at the age of twenty-one, meets Aurélien de Sèze, a young judge from Bordeaux and falls in love with him. They exchange love letters for several years and see each other a few times up until 1830.

   November: After a period of great stress Aurore tells her husband about her interest in Aurélien de Sèze and calls for "household peace," stipulating its conditions in writing.

1826 Stays in Paris and in Nohant. Aurore tells Zoé Leroy, her friend and confidente, that Stéphane Ajasson de Grandsagne has returned to Nohant. She becomes very fond of the young scholar, who gave her natural history lessons in Nohant in years past.

1827 August: A short trip to Auvergne. Various health problems.

   December: On the pretext of medical consultations, Aurore goes to Paris to be with Stéphane Ajasson de Grandsagne.

1828 13 September: Solange is born. Her father is most likely Stéphane Ajasson de Grandsagne.

1829 Aurore writes travel memories, *La marraine*, and an unfinished text, *Histoire d'un rêveur*. A few brief stays in southwest France, in particular, at Guillery, at the house of Casimir Dudevant's father.

1830 July: Aurore meets Jules Sandeau, seven years her junior, who is dreaming of becoming a writer. She soon becomes his mistress.

   November: After violent quarrels Casimir Dudevant accepts that his wife will henceforth spend six months of the year in Paris.

1831 Aurore moves to 25 quai Saint-Michel. Maurice, who is eight years old, is entrusted to the care of a tutor, Jules Boucoiran, while Solange, who is three, stays at Nohant with her father.

Aurore briefly thinks about decorating Spa boxes to earn a living. Henri de Latouche (or Delatouche) asks her to write a few articles for a satirical paper, the *Figaro*. With or without the help of Jules Sandeau, she publishes a few short stories *(La prima donna, La fille d'Albano)*, then a novel, *Rose et Blanche ou La comédienne et la religieuse*, that they sign together with the pseudonym "J. Sand."

1832   May: Publication of *Indiana*, which Aurore wrote at Nohant the previous winter. The novel is signed "G. Sand."*

October: She breaks up with Jules Sandeau and moves to 19 quai Malaquais. This time Solange is with her. She publishes two short stories, *Melchior* and *La marquise*.

November: Sand publishes her second novel, *Valentine*.

December: Sand's only poem in verse, *La reine Mab*, and *Le toast* are published. She agrees to collaborate on a regular basis with the prestigious *Revue des Deux Mondes*, directed by François Buloz.

1833   January: Sand meets Marie Dorval, a great star of Romantic theater, and becomes passionately involved with her. She publishes some short stories, *Cora, Une vieille histoire*, then *Aldo le rimeur* and *Métella*.

Spring: She meets Alfred de Musset at a dinner. They begin writing to each other.

July: Sand becomes Musset's mistress. She has just published *Lélia* and been harshly criticized by the press.

December: The lovers leave for Italy.

1834   Their stay in Venice soon turns to drama. Sand falls ill with dysentery, then Musset gets typhoid fever with attacks of delirium. Dr. Luigi Pagello, who was called to treat Musset, becomes Sand's lover.

Late March: Musset leaves Italy. Sand spends the next three months in Venice, then decides to go back to Paris with Pagello in order to see her children.

July: She leaves Pagello and goes back to Musset. The couple separates once again a few weeks later. *Le secrétaire intime*, *Jacques*, and *Léone Léoni* are published in installments in the *Revue des Deux Mondes*. *Garnier* and four open letters are published in a volume entitled *Lettres d'un voyageur*.

1835   Sand and Musset become lovers once again.

March: They break up once and for all. Sand returns to Nohant and meets the lawyer Michel who will be her lover until the spring of 1837. She also becomes friends with Félicité de Lamennais and Pierre Leroux, a socialist thinker to whom she will give financial support for years. Her political sympathies, republican and socialist, are becoming clearer. The *Revue des Deux Mondes* publishes *André* and three new open letters.

1836 The legal separation between Sand and her husband keeps the first months of the year busy.

Late July: A final judgment gives Sand back all the property she owned at the time of her wedding and awards her custody of the children.

Late August: She goes to Chamonix with Maurice and Solange. There she meets up with Franz Liszt and Marie d'Agoult. She publishes *Simon*, *Poème de Myrza*, *Mattéa*, and *Le Dieu inconnu*.

1837 February–March: Franz Liszt and Marie d'Agoult come to stay at Nohant.

May–July: Franz Liszt and Marie d'Agoult once again stay at Nohant.

Sand publishes *Lettres d'un voyageur*, *Mauprat*, and *Les maîtres mosaïstes*. She also publishes some open letters in Lamennais's paper, *Le Monde* (they will be published as a volume entitled *Lettres à Marcie*), but Lamennais refuses to publish her defense of divorce.

1838 Winter: Balzac spends a week at Nohant.

June: Sand becomes the mistress of Frédéric Chopin, age twenty-eight, and they will spend nine years together.

October: The lovers decide to go to Spain along with Sand's children.

December: After their arrival in Majorca, they settle in at the charterhouse of Valldemosa where they spend only a few weeks because of Chopin's health and the uncomfortable quarters. Sand publishes in installments *La dernière Aldini*, *L'Uscoque*, and *Spiridion* as well as the short story *L'orco*.

1839 Summer: Sand is at Nohant with Chopin.

October: Sand moves to an apartment in rue Pigalle, in Paris. She publishes a new version of *Lélia*. The *Revue des Deux Mondes* publishes *Gabriel*, *Pauline* et *Les sept cordes de la lyre*.

1840   April: Sand ventures into theater for the first time with *Cosima*, a failure. She meets Agricol Perdiguier, compagnon du Devoir in Avignon and author of the *Livre du compagnonnage* (1839). Sand's *Le compagnon du tour de Fra*nce, which draws on Perdiguier's work, is published as a book in December.

1841   Sand publishes articles under the title *Un hiver au midi de l'Europe* (these articles will be published all together the following year under the title *Un hiver à Majorque*) and *Mouny-Robin*.

   July: Sand breaks off all professional dealings with François Buloz after a disagreement about her novel *Horace*, which the director of the *Revue des Deux Mondes* found too ideological.

   November: The first issue of the *Revue Indépendante*, founded by Sand, Pierre Leroux, and Louis Viardot, the husband of the opera singer Pauline Garcia, is published.

1842   May–September: Sand is in Nohant. The painter Eugène Delacroix, in whose studio Maurice is working as an apprentice, makes a visit.

   October: Sand and Chopin return to Paris; they settle respectively at 5 and 9 square d'Orléans. *La Revue Indépendante* begins publishing *Consuelo*.

1843   Late spring, summer, and fall: Sand is in Nohant, entertaining in particular Louis and Pauline Viardot as well as Eugène Delacroix. *La Revue Indépendante* continues publishing *Consuelo*, then the sequel, *La comtesse de Rudolstadt*, plus various articles. *Kourroglou*, *Jean Ziska*, and *Carl* are published in magazines. Sand publishes a brochure in defense of "Fanchette," a young mentally handicapped woman. This signals her entry into politics.

1844   Another stay of several months at Nohant.

   September: The first issue of *L'Éclaireur: Journal des Départements de l'Indre, du Cher et de la Creuse*, founded by Sand and socialist friends of hers, is published. In this paper she publishes several articles about the situation of peasants and criticizes the government's policies. *Jeanne* is published in installments along with various little pieces in prose.

1845   June–December: Sand is in Nohant with Chopin and receives a number of guests. Two of her "socialist" novels, *Le meunier d'Angibault* and *Le péché de monsieur Antoine*, are published in installments. *Isidora* and *Teverino* are also published. The writer and publisher Pierre Hetzel works as Sand's literary agent, negotiating contracts and making sure that her numerous publications in books and magazines run smoothly (he goes into exile in Brussels after the coup d'état in December 1851).

1846   May: Sand settles in at Nohant and stays there until February of the following year. Chopin accompanies her.

November: Chopin leaves Nohant for good. Solange turns eighteen and is courted by Fernand de Préaulx.

December: Sand puts on her first play for the parlor-theater at Nohant, and this one is followed by many others. The various roles are played by members of the family, friends, and servants. Costumes and decors are made by the group. *La mare au diable* and *Lucrezia Floriani* are published in installments.

1847   February: Sand and Solange pose in the studio of Jean-Baptiste (a.k.a. Auguste) Clésinger, who sculpts busts of the two. Solange falls in love with the artist and breaks things off with Fernand de Préaulx.

May: Solange's wedding, despite Sand's reservations, is celebrated on 19 May.

July: A violent scene about money occurs between Sand, Maurice, and the Clésingers, husband and wife. The sculptor threatens Sand with his gun. Chopin defends Solange and breaks things off with Sand by letter. *Il piccinino* is published in installments, along with several articles and reviews in various newspapers and magazines.

1848   When the February Revolution breaks out, George Sand goes to Paris and meets up with her friends in the provisional government, including Louis Blanc, Armand Barbès, and Ledru-Rollin. She publishes various brochures at her own expense and participates in writing issues of the *Bulletin de la République*. She founds a newspaper, *La Cause du Peuple*, and also writes in *La Vraie République* of Théophile Thoré. Her prologue, *Le roi attend*, opens at the Théâtre-Français, renamed Théâtre de la République.

March: Sand crosses paths for the last time with Frédéric Chopin, who tells her that Solange has given birth to a little girl, Jeanne-Gabrielle, who will live only a few days.

May: Dismayed to witness the failure of the socialist republic she so desired, Sand returns to Nohant.

June: The June Days, during which the demonstrations of workers are severely repressed, brings her to total despair. Two of her most famous novels, *François le Champi* and *La petite fadette*, are published as serials.

1849   Sand spends most of her time at Nohant, only going to Paris from time to time, as she will continue to do for the rest of her life.

September: Solange's second daughter, Jeanne Clésigner, nicknamed Nini, is born.

17 October: Chopin dies.

November: The stage adaptation of *François le Champi* is a great success at the Odéon Theater. Alexandre Manceau, engraver and friend of Maurice, moves into the château of Nohant. He is thirty-one and will share Sand's life until his death in 1865.

1850   Summer: Numerous visitors at Nohant. The theater activities continue, especially the puppet theater. Sand takes part in writing sketches, plus making costumes and props. *Histoire du véritable gribouille* is published.

1851   February: The parlor theater of Nohant is inaugurated.

September: The *Œuvres illustrées* of Sand, published jointly by Blanchard, Hetzel, and Marescq, begin appearing. Tony Johannot and Maurice Sand are the illustrators. *Le château des désertes* is published. *Claudie* opens at the Théâtre de la Porte-Saint-Martin, *Molière* at the Théâtre de la Gaîté, and *Le mariage de Victorine* at the Théâtre du Gymnase.

1852   January: Sand meets in Paris with Louis-Napoléon Bonaparte, who, after the coup d'état of 2 December 1851, ordered that many political opponents be arrested and deported. Sand obtains pardons and reduced sentences for many of them.

February: Sand meets Prince Jérôme Napoléon, who brings together republicans and moderate liberals (the prince will become the godfather of Sand's granddaughter, Aurore).

June: Solange and her daughter arrive in Nohant.

August: When Solange leaves Nohant, she entrusts her daughter to her mother. *Les vacances de Pandolfe*, followed by *Le démon du foyer*, opens at the Théâtre du Gymnase. *Mont-Revêche* and various articles are published in installments.

1853 To ensure her children's financial future Sand tries to sell her "literary property," meaning her future royalties. She spends a good part of the year dealing with various publishers, without success. *Le pressoir* opens at the Théâtre du Gymnase, then a stage adaptation of *Mauprat* is mounted at the Odéon. *La filleule* and *Les maîtres sonneurs* are published in installments.

1854 May: Jean-Baptiste Clésinger, now separated from his wife, comes to Nohant to get Nini and demands custody of the little girl. *Flaminio* opens at the Théâtre du Gymnase.

5 October: Installments of *Adriani* start appearing. *La Presse*, a newspaper founded by Émile de Girardin in 1836, begins publishing *Histoire de ma vie*. Sand's autobiography will appear in 138 installments; at the same time, the publisher Lecou guarantees its publication in book form: twenty volumes appear between 1854 and 1855.

1855 Just when Sand obtains custody of her granddaughter Nini, the little girl dies of scarlet fever in Paris. She is buried at Nohant, next to Sand's father and grandmother. In March Sand, Manceau, and Maurice leave Nohant for three months in Italy (Maurice leaves lots of drawings of the trip). Sand stays for several weeks in a villa in Frascati. *Le maître Favilla* opens at the Odéon. *Le diable aux champs* is published. Sand signs a contract with the publisher Hachette for ten novels in the collection *Bibliothèque des chemins de fer*.

1856 Performances at the theater in Nohant continue in full swing. The amateur actors, and sometimes professional actors from Paris, improvise in part under Sand's direction. *Lucie* and then *Françoise* open at the Théâtre du Gymnase as well as a stage adaptation of *Comme il vous plaira* at the Comédie-Française. There is a new production of *Claudie* at the Odéon, and this will be the only one of Sand's plays to be performed on a regular basis up through the nineteenth century. *Évenor* and *Leucippe* are published in installments.

May: Sand changes her penmanship in order to write more quickly and to give her publishers more legible manuscripts.

1857 July: Manceau buys a little house in the village of Gargilesse, in Creuse. The couple will often stay there for short periods of time. In 1864, Manceau will sell the house to Maurice, subject to usufruct. *La Daniella*, *Les dames vertes*, and *Les beaux messieurs de Bois-Doré* are published in installments.

1858   After years of conflict François Buloz reconciles with Sand and agrees to publish *L'homme de neige* in the *Revue des Deux Mondes*. *Narcisse* is published in installments. *Légendes rustiques* is published by Morel, with illustrations by Maurice, to whom the work is dedicated.

1859   *Elle et lui*, a fictional version of Sand's affair with Musset, is published in installments. Musset published his own version in *La confession d'un enfant du siècle* in 1836. Defending his brother who had died two years before, Paul de Musset retorts by publishing *Lui et elle*. Louise Colet, Musset's last mistress, does the same with *Lui*. *Marguerite de Saint-Gemme* opens at the Théâtre du Gymnase. *Flavie, Jean de la Roche*, and *Constance Verrier* are published in installments.

   May: Sand has her first contacts with Michel Lévy, who will soon become her nearly exclusive publisher.

   September: *Masques et bouffons*, written and illustrated by Maurice Sand, with a preface by George Sand, is published.

   December: The perfume manufacturer Henri Rafin launches an "Eau de George Sand for the body and the hanky."

1860   Early March: Sand is in Paris and meets her writer friends, including the young Gustave Flaubert. She visits the Pompei-style house that Prince Jérôme had built for himself on the Champs-Elysées.

   Summer: Sand is particularly busy, writing numerous sketches for the theater of Nohant.

   Fall: Sand falls ill with typhoid fever and gallbladder problems that leave her feeling very weak. *La ville noire* and *Le marquis de Villemer* are published in installments. Four volumes of Sand's *Théâtre*, with a selection of plays written over a period of more than ten years, are published.

1861   February–May: Sand convalesces in Tamaris, near Toulon, with Manceau, Maurice, and Marie Caillaud, a maid and much appreciated actress in the parlor-theater of Nohant. Maurice leaves an album of drawings of this trip.

   Fall: Sand is again at loggerheads with Solange whom she has accused of being a kept woman. For the next four years Solange writes no letters to her mother. To Alexandre Dumas fils, a regular visitor to Nohant, Sand confesses her feelings for the painter Charles Marchal. She is fifty-seven, and he is thirty-six. They have a brief exchange of love letters. *Valvèdre* and *La famille de Germandre* are published in installments.

1862   17 May: Maurice, age thirty-nine, weds Lina Calamatta, age twenty, daughter of the engraver Luigi Calamatta, a longtime friend, in a civil wedding ceremony. The following year they are married in a Protestant ceremony. Eugène Fromentin has a brief stay in Nohant. The family and friends spend time at Gargilesse, walking in the countryside to better their knowledge of plants, minerals, and insects and writing sketches for the parlor theater. *Pavé* opens at the Théâtre du Gymnase, followed by the stage adaptation of *Les beaux messieurs de Bois-*Doré at the Ambigu-Comique. *Tamaris* and *Antonia* are published in installments; two collections of articles, *Autour de la table* and *Souvenirs et impressions littéraires*, are published in book form. Sand writes the preface for Maurice's *Six mille lieues à toute vapeur*, a narrative about his trip to America on Prince Jérôme's yacht.

1863   14 July: Marc-Antoine, the son of Maurice and Lina, is born. He will die of dysentery a year later.

November: Maurice expresses his wish to see Manceau leave Nohant. Sand decides to follow her companion. *Mademoiselle La Quintinie*, a critique of the way confession is practiced at the time in the Roman Catholic Church, is published in installments. Because of this book Sand's complete works are put on the Index Librorum Prohibitorum.

1864   February: The stage adaptation of *Le marquis de Villemer* opens at the Odéon, and Sand is enthusiastically hailed.

June: Sand and Manceau settle in a villa surrounded by a garden that they bought in Palaiseau. The house will be sold in 1869. They keep a pied-à-terre in Paris. *Drac* opens at the Théâtre du Vaudeville. A selection of Nohant's parlor theater, *Le théâtre de Nohant*, is published. *Laura* and *La confession d'une jeune fille* are published in installments.

1865   18 August: Alexandre Manceau, who has had tuberculosis for several years, dies in Palaiseau after protracted suffering. *Monsieur Sylvestre* and a short story, *La coupe*, are published in installments.

1866   10 January: Aurore, the daughter of Maurice and Lina, is born in Nohant.

February: On a trip to Paris Sand goes for the first time to dinner at Magny's, a monthly event for writers that Sainte-Beuve organized in 1863. She becomes friends with Gustave Flaubert. *Don Juan de village* and *Lys du Japon*, a stage adaptation of *Antonia*, open at the Théâtre du Vaudeville. Sand travels to Brittany and stays with Flaubert at Croisset. *Le dernier amour* is published in installments, and *Promenades autour d'un village* is published in book form. Sand writes the preface for Maurice's *Le monde des papillons*.

1867 Sand goes back to live at Nohant. In September she has two briefs stays in Normandy in order to write *Mademoiselle Merquem*. *Cadio* is published in installments. Maurice publishes *Le coq aux cheveux d'or*.

1868 Winter: Sand travels to the French Riviera and stays with Juliette Adam in Bruyères.

11 March: Gabrielle, the second daughter of Maurice and Lina, is born at Nohant.

May: After a brief stay with Flaubert in Croisset, Sand visits the Art Salon at the Louvre where she admires paintings by Marchal, Daubigny, Fromentin, and Gérôme. Sand moves for the last time in Paris, to 5 rue Gay-Lussac. *Mademoiselle Merquem* and a few articles that will be part of the collection *Nouvelles lettres d'un voyageur* are published in installments.

1869 Spring: While visiting Paris, Sand poses for Félix Nadar. Wearing a striped shawl, she is sixty-five years old.

Fall: Sand makes two short trips to the Ardennes with friends. Flaubert comes to spend the last days of the year at Nohant. *Pierre qui roule* and *Lupo Liverani* are published in installments.

1870 September: Fleeing from a smallpox epidemic, Sand and family, who are also fearing that the Prussians will arrive in Berry, take refuge with friends in Creuse. *L'autre* opens at the Odéon. *Malgrétout* and *Césarine Dietrich* are published in installments. Against her mother's advice, Solange publishes *Jacques Bruneau* (she will publish a second novel, *Carl Robert*, in 1884).

1871 March: Sand severely criticizes the Paris Commune, even though she condemned the bloody repression that followed. *Francia* and the *Journal d'un voyageur pendant la guerre* are published in installments.

August: Sand becomes a regular collaborator of the news-paper *Le Temps*.

1872 Summer: Sand stays in Cabourg with her granddaughters.

Fall: Sand entertains the Viardot family and Ivan Turgenev. *Nanon, Un bienfait n'est jamais perdu*, and her first stories for children are published in installments. These stories will later appear under the title *Contes d'une grand-mère*.

1873 April: Flaubert, then the Viardot family and Turgenev visit Nohant. Solange buys the château of Montgivray. A few kilo-meters from Nohant, it once belonged to Hippolyte Chatiron.

August: Trip to Auvergne.

September: The Viardot family and Turgenev return to Nohant. *Impressions et souvenirs* and *Contes d'une grand-mère*, dedicated to Gabrielle and Aurore, are published.

1874 Sand's health is deteriorating. After trying her hand at den-dritic painting, she spends the winter using this technique with Maurice.

December: Maurice is elected mayor of the commune of Nohant-Vicq (he was also mayor for a few weeks in 1848). *Ma sœur Jeanne* is published.

1875 During the winter Sand, who is planning a new edition of her complete works with Michel Lévy, organizes what she has written and composes a general preface. *Flamarande, Marianne Chevreuse*, and *La tour de Percemont*, plus a new series of stories, are published in installments.

1876 Winter: Sand starts her last novel, *Albine Fiori*, which will remain unfinished.

*All of Sand's published works are listed here, except for brochures, arti-cles, prefaces, and many reviews of works. The works are dated with the time of their publication as newspaper installments or magazines or, in some rare cases, just as books. Her plays are listed with the date of their first performance.

George Sand? Just hearing the name of one of the most famous women in French literature, people, even today, readily express their admiration or aggravation. They really love her or they don't like her much at all; they can't get enough of her novels or they basically ignore them. Most people seem to fall in the second category. Take a look at the current literary histories or manuals for high school and university students in France, and you'll see that Sand continues to occupy a modest place, her work often being reduced to a few "rustic" novels. Yet her place should be right beside the other literary giant of the time, Victor Hugo. Both produced a huge corpus and were eager to make literature a space for moral and political commitment; both exercised the same vibrant influence over the intellectual life of France for nearly half a century, demonstrating the same vigilant care for society and the lower classes, in short, the same way of being in the world, bountiful and generous.

Half admiring, half tongue in cheek, Gustave Flaubert gladly referred to "Mama Sand" and "Papa Hugo," making these two the symbolic parents of every author in the second half of the nineteenth century, and his own for starters. Yet the way the two of them are treated is quite different, and the same goes for the place reserved to each in France's literary tradition, the way that these men, women, and the books they wrote are generally remembered. There are all kinds of reasons for this, having to do with their sex, how being a man or a woman conditioned the way they got into literature, the course of their careers, the reception given to their works at the time of publication, and their reputation for posterity. Hugo, whom Sand never met, with whom she had more political affinities than literary ones, no doubt found the best words for sizing up the importance of the woman who was just two years shy of being his exact contemporary. For her funeral in June 1876 he wrote: "George Sand has a unique place in our time. The others are great men; she is the great woman. It is this century's duty to complete the French Revolution and to start the human revolution, sexual equality being part of mankind's equality, and so there had to be a great woman. . . . This is how the revolution is fulfilled."[1]

Yet the majority of France's "great men" did not share this point of view and would not for quite a while. They preferred to see Sand as "an error of Nature,"[2] unsettling by virtue of her genius or frankly ridiculous by dint of her ambitions to genius. They were revolted by her singularly free behavior that kept the contradictions inherent in private life separate from the convictions that she expressed again and again in her particularly abundant and varied works. More fundamentally perhaps, they were thoroughly annoyed to see a woman abandon her role as muse, mother, as giver of inspiration or consolation, in order to do just what they did. "Bluestocking," they bellowed, "housekeeper," "sleepwalker," "big silly," "show-off," "a non-genius," "a she-ghoul," "a latrine," "a ruminating sphinx," "the Prudhomme[3] of immorality," "the mum of mush," "the plague of the Republic," "the Marquis de Sade's daughter," "the novel-writing cow."

The period's misogyny was not limited to this deluge of insults. It also churned out loads of caricatures making fun of the woman wearing pants, smoking cigars, dreaming about a "Chamber of Female Representatives," and spinning her literary yarns among a flock of sheep. Honoré Daumier's series called *The Bluestockings* [*Les bas-bleus*] took aim at the women who wanted to imitate Sand, dreaming of writing novels and, in the meantime, refusing to sew the buttons back on their husband's trousers. Literary criticism quickly got tangled up in contradictions. Either Sand was mediocre, because she "is a woman and will remain one forever"[4] (Zola), and there's always been "something very homey about her, like a *pot-roast*"[5] (Maupassant); from that point on she amounted to "the greatest prejudice of our time, the century's most routine exercise of admiration"[6] (Barbey). Or, on the other hand, Sand was a genius.

In this case, however, "she's a man and all the more man that she wants to be one and has stepped out of a woman's role"[7] (Balzac); "a woman made man," her talent having made a monster out of her: if she's not "that hermaphrodite genius that brings together a man's vigor and a woman's grace"[8] (Dumas), she belongs to some "third sex"[9] (Flaubert).

Endowed with this "narrative genius"[10] hailed by Flaubert, acting as the tireless advocate of the "great forces in charge of the world,"[11] according to Taine, resolute in politics, courageous in the defense of women and peasants, always endeavoring to be perfectly independent in tone, behavior, and expression, Sand had a complicated personality, and the history of her life is no less complicated. Her works, novels, and plays, autobiographical writings and correspondence, reflect this, but like a mirror in a funhouse. In her works Sand undergoes dizzying metamorphoses: "Where would art be, great God! if one not did invent three-quarters of the characters, magnifying their beauty or ugliness, traits in which the stupid and curious public wants to recognize the people they were modeled on?"[12] she asks. For the same reason, the life of the woman who chose to hide under the masculine mask of "George Sand" to get herself into literature and make a name for herself there only sheds light on part of her extremely varied production, and vice versa.

This biography does not aim to account for all of the many lives and publications that made of Sand an extraordinary woman and a woman of letters. Its purpose is more modest: to put forth a series of observations that will allow the reader to size up an exceptional personality and fount of creativity and at the same time to refute a few die-hard clichés. Any attempt to talk about all the years of Sand's life, the men and women who crossed her path, the books she wrote, and the causes she defended could only take the form of a painting with some spots only sketched out. This will be an unfinished portrait of a *great* woman, but a portrait rich with suggestions about a milieu, a moment, and a singular destiny.

"She has died, here now she lives," Victor Hugo proclaimed in the funeral oration already quoted. The old man knew how to find just the right words. The same words apply here. After many other attempts at Sand's biography, it is now a matter of breathing life back into Aurore who became George, Madame Dudevant who all of a sudden became Madame Sand one fine day in May 1832—and of telling her fascinating story.

Before May 1832 "George Sand" did not exist, or more precisely she existed under another name. Her first name was Aurore, she was twenty-seven and married to Casimir Dudevant, a country gentleman from Quercy, in southwestern France. "Dark eyes, dark hair, ordinary forehead, pale complexion, well-formed nose, round chin, average mouth, five feet tall, with no particular identifying marks,"[1] she noted in *Story of My Life* [*Histoire de ma vie*], judging that she had been "neither ugly nor beautiful"[2] in her youth. She was living in the château of Nohant, a mile or two from La Châtre, some twenty-five miles south of Châteauroux, in the central French province of Berry. She dressed with a certain elegance, and the neighbors who had watched her grow up thought her a rather strange and unpredictable young woman. She was bored or else lost in dreams, by turns wildly amused or deeply sad. Her two children, Maurice and Solange, were eight and three.

During the summer of 1830, at the château of Coudray, owned by her friends the Duvernets, she met a frail young man with blond hair and a sweet look about him. She penciled his portrait. Seven years her junior, Jules Sandeau aspired to be a man of letters. Aurore Dudevant, having become his mistress, planned to move to Paris with him. They in fact did so the following January when the lovers settled down together at 21 quai des Grands-Augustins. After bitter rows (and a history of discord and infidelity already rather long), Casimir Dudevant agreed to let his wife spend a few months a year away from Nohant and gave her an allowance from the income of the estate he continued to manage. She gave him temporary custody of their two children.

Hoping to pad her purse a bit, the young woman first thought about decorating screens, snuff boxes, and Spa boxes, which took their name from the famous Belgian resort that launched the fashion of these little hand-painted souvenir chests. But others were better at varnishing the pansies, daisies, and lilies of the valley painted in delicate gouache colors. Her boxes didn't move from the shopwindow. With the help of her friends from Berry, she soon met Henri Delatouche (or de Latouche), a cousin of the Duvernets and the editor of the *Figaro*, a little satirical paper, and he invited her to publish texts of her choice in that venue.

Aurore Dudevant had already been thinking about writing for some time. Like all the young ladies of her class, she had written long letters to her friends from boarding school, but from the very start hers were far livelier than those of her correspondents, funnier as well. In the past she had tried describing the countryside around Nohant, drafted memories of a few trips with her husband, and penned some sketches of people who were part of her daily life. In a short text entitled *Cuttings* [*Les couperies*] dated 3 September 1830, she had imagined a face-to-face confrontation between a young man and an old woman. Through a sort of fantastic projection of what her future held in store, this piece summed up an entire life, her joys and sorrows, hopes and disappointments, dreams of faraway places and the separations that necessarily occur when these dreams are realized.

But writing is not just finding words for one's moods, memories, or flights of fancy. With Jules Sandeau, Aurore Dudevant was discovering the life of journalists paid by the line, writing all together under the supervision of a newspaper director watching over every detail and keeping everybody busy. As she relayed to her son's tutor, Jules Boucoiran, on 4 March 1831, "We are not exactly *free*, at the *Figaro*. M. Delatouche, our *worthy* boss . . . orders us around, pruning, hacking away, imposing his fancies, whims, and odd notions. And we've got to write the way he wants. After all, it's his business and we're just his unskilled laborers: a *news-worker*, a *junior staff-writer*, that's me for the moment."[3]

Still in conjunction with Sandeau, she wrote several short stories that appeared in the *Figaro* but also *La Mode* and *La Revue de Paris*. They had to write lots and quickly: "*Writers* (says the

sublime Latouche) are tools . . . , not men, but pens!"[4] The young couple
even agreed to write a counterfeit novel entitled *Le commissaire*,
presented by the publisher Renault as the posthumous work of
Alphonse Signol, killed in a duel a short time before.

On Delatouche's suggestion, Aurore Dudevant and Jules
Sandeau signed their first texts as "J. S." or "J. Sand," sharing this
slight modification of the young man's last name as one pen name
for the two of them.[5] Women singers, passionate artists, and gentlemen involved in rather tormented love affairs were their staple.
Such characters and subjects were fashionable, terribly melodra-
matic sentimental novels still being all the rage, and publishers
were soliciting them from every writer eager to earn some money.
In December 1831 Jules Sandeau and Aurore Dudevant published
another novel, *Rose and Blanche, or the Actress and the Nun* [*Rose et
Blanche ou La comédienne et la religieuse*]. Signed "J. Sand," this one
drew the attention of the critics.

All the young men dreaming of a literary career at that time
started out more or less the same way. While waiting for their
first work to get published, they would agree to be ghostwriters or
assistants for a book publisher or newspaper editor, generally for a
press whose growing success would altogether change the literary
landscape for years to come. Literature was becoming "industrial."
So said Sainte-Beuve in an article written in 1839. This would
cause a radical change in the *trade*, turning authors into chroniclers
and novelists who would first publish their works in a newspaper
or magazine, then in book form. Nearly all the great authors of the
time worked this way.

In those years there were very few women in the press or literary establishment. The reasons for this are complex and go far back
in time. Women had been writing for centuries, but always as a
minority, and their talents were generally tolerated as an exception.
The shapers of opinion, from medieval clerics to Enlightenment
philosophers, had always repeated that no decent woman could
tolerate the publicity of publication: once her work reached the
man in the street, the female author became a "public" woman, no
more and no less than actresses and prostitutes, an old adage that

Baudelaire would see fit to repeat. Likewise, for hundreds of years there had been men, admittedly few in number, who encouraged women to learn, write, and publish and not to content themselves with age-old arguments about their "natural" inferiority and the supposed superiority of the "strong" sex. And for hundreds of years, women had been thinking about their place in literature, highlighting the difficulties of their situation and their unfriendly treatment at the hands of the critics. With this in mind, they sometimes invited their sisters of the pen to sacrifice some vain dream of glory to the joys of marriage and family; fortunately, they sometimes exhorted them to write poems, plays, and novels, to surrender to the giddy excitement of creation. Tradition, being rather stingy in its compliments, quite agreed that these women had more than enough imagination.

After the Revolution, more women began publishing. The number of female novelists alone doubled, probably represent-ing 20 percent of the published authors at the time. During the Restoration (1815–1830) the popularity of sentimental novels even put a handful of women writers on the best-seller list, for exam-ple, Sophie Cottin, whose novels *Claire d'Albe* and *Elizabeth or the Siberian Exiles* [*Claire of Alba* and *Elisabeth ou les exilées de Sibérie*] are completely forgotten today, like many other publications that enjoyed real success at that time.

The greater visibility of women authors explains the increased hostility shown them. In the 1830s the English term *bluestocking*, translated as *bas-bleu*, was making the rounds. A rallying point for lampoonists, it helped make a laughing stock out of any woman with literary or intellectual ambitions. Poking fun at learned, pre-cious, or pretentious women of any sort was far from over. On this particular point Molière had made an enduring mark. When the "George Sand" story began in the first years of the July Monarchy (1830–1848), the prejudices about women and literature or, more generally, artistic creation were firmly entrenched.

The Napoleonic Civil Code of 1804 had more strictly defined the place of men and women: the public sphere was for men, and the private sphere for women. Divorce had been abolished in 1816, soon after the Bourbon monarchy returned to power. The Catholic Church again took control of the schools, especially those for girls, who would mainly be taught to keep house and be mothers. They needed some instruction, since they would be their children's first teachers. *Virtue, discretion, honesty, courage, resignation,* and *self-denial* were the keywords of the short catechism for girls. The great minds of the time proclaimed that the future of France and the nation's moral standards depended on women being indoctrinated in this catalogue of virtues. Each sex had its role, place, and prescribed behavior. Men were to be virile, and women sweet and submissive, yet flirtatious enough to attract a future husband. No woman's life would be considered successful without a husband and his children. Men commanded, as the judicial system bluntly stated, and women obeyed. Fortunately, there was real life, and couples enjoying mutual love and desire could shake up that mass of constraints in thousands of ways.

Still a writer had to be free to move about in a way quite unimaginable for a woman. Every fledging author was not only duty bound to live in Paris, as young Sandeau and many others knew so well, but to run around the streets at any hour, frequent cafés and theaters, slip into the backrooms of bookshops, the newsroom of a magazine or newspaper, a theater director's office. Going out unaccompanied and showing up alone in public were more complicated for a woman than one would think. There were constraints everywhere, each sex had its own place, and both were sternly enjoined to stay within those bounds. So a woman had to justify her presence in the street by displaying the reasons for it, by wearing, for example, the distinctive dress of a landlady, servant, seamstress, milliner's assistant, or some other form of women's work in order not to be mistaken for a prostitute. A lady could only go out chaperoned, by a maid, if necessary. Her reputation, and that of her father, brother, or husband, were at stake.

So it comes as no surprise that Aurore Dudevant, having had ample opportunity to sample the reproving looks and wagging tongues of the small-town bourgeoisie of La Châtre, decided to dress as a man. That meant that she could move around discreetly without exciting gossip, go to theaters and concerts without being accosted or attracting unwanted attention. What liberty these gentlemen in trousers and frock coats enjoyed!

> I saw my young friends from Berry, my childhood chums, living in Paris. Broke like me, they still managed to keep up with everything that appealed to intelligent young men. Literary and political happenings, the excitement of theaters and museums, clubs and street life, they were seeing everything, going everywhere. . . . But on the streets of Paris I was like a boat on ice. My delicate shoes would split after two days, . . . I didn't know how to lift up my hem, I was a filthy mess, worn out, sick with colds, and watching shoes and dresses, not to mention dainty velvet hats drenched by rain spouts, turn into tatters at a terrifying clip.[6]

Her mother suggested that she dress as a man. That is what she, like so many others, had done in her youth. It made everything easier and saved money.

> First off I found this idea funny and then really ingenious. I had been dressed as a boy in my childhood, then I had hunted wearing a smock frock and gaiters . . . , so I wasn't at all amazed to start dressing again in a way that was nothing new for me. Fashion just then made it particularly easy to go about in disguise. Men were wearing long, boxy frock coats "*à la propriétaire*," going down to the heels and without any waistline. Once when my brother was putting his on at Nohant, he laughed and said, "Really nice, don't you think? . . . The tailor measures up a sentry-box, and it would fit an entire regiment just fine." I had one made for myself, plus a pair of trousers and a vest, all in coarse grey material. With a grey hat and bulky wool necktie, I was a perfect little first-year university student. . . . I would fly from one end of Paris to the other. . . . I saw every play from the orchestra pit. . . . I was too poorly dressed and looked too unsophisticated—my usual way, absentminded and often dazed—to attract anyone's attention.[7]

And so Aurore Dudevant entered literature—on tiptoe. While she took male disguise to enjoy perfect freedom of movement, just like her old friends from Berry, she also hid behind her lover's initials or truncated last name. That was the great difference between Sandeau and his companion. More than fifty years later, Gabrielle-Sidonie Colette started her literary career quite the same way. She allowed her husband, the influential Henri Gauthier-Villars, to sign her first novels with the sole name "Willy" and let herself be photographed dressed as Claudine, the character of the libertine schoolgirl in her novel, sitting at the feet of her master along with her dog Toby-chien.

After this trying début in the offices of the *Figaro*, she could have just given up. Such was not the case. Back in Nohant in the fall of 1831, she started a novel whose title was drawn from the first name of her heroine, Indiana. The narration opens on a tedious country evening: "On a cool and rainy autumn evening three people in a little castle down in Brie were seriously occupied. Lost in thought, they were watching the embers smoldering in the hearth and the clock's hands proceeding along their slow march."[8] Unhappily married, Indiana falls in love with another man and winds up leaving her husband. But her lover is fickle, and it seems impossible to overcome the force of prejudice. Finally, the young woman and her childhood friend Ralph who has fallen in love with her decide to commit suicide by jumping off a cliff. This last chapter is followed by a "conclusion" in which a traveler comes upon the young couple leading a quiet life on the isle of Bourbon. Instead of the existential brick wall leading to suicide, the author finally preferred a kind of mythic retreat inspired by Bernardin de Saint-Pierre's *Paul et Virginie*.

Indiana is not just another of the many romances that women tended to write—love being the feeling women know best, or so it is said. The novel describes and takes a stand against the condition of married women's lives and, more generally, of society itself: "If the writer, while carrying out his task, has happened to voice complaints wrung out of his characters by the social problems affecting them; if he has not been afraid to repeat their aspirations for a better life, let the inequalities of society and the whims of destiny bear the blame! Writers are just a mirror that reflects these problems, a machine that reproduces them."[9]

Using masculine pronouns to refer to herself throughout this work, Aurore Dudevant insisted on spelling out this message in a carefully argued preface. A writer was born, and this first work is certainly a masterpiece that seems to have required remarkably little preparation. Aside from bits and pieces of various manuscripts, there are few early works[10] or expressions of ambition for a literary career. Glory? Fame? Just a few months earlier, Aurore Dudevant was poking fun at this idea as something perfectly improbable, as she wrote to Jules Boucoiran: "My husband has given me an allowance of 3,000 francs. . . . So I only wish to increase my comfort by turning a little profit, and since I have no ambition for fame, I won't be famous. . . . So when people come tell me that glory is yet more trouble that I'm preparing for myself, I can't help laughing at the word, not at all felicitous, and all the stereotypes that apply only to genius or vanity. I've got neither one nor the other."[11]

A writer was born, but what about her name? Was Aurore Dudevant going to keep the pseudonym "J. Sand" that Delatouche had given her?

> I had written *Indiana* at Nohant; I wanted to sign it with the popular pseudonym, but Jules Sandeau, out of modesty, did not want to accept fathering a book that was totally alien to him. That didn't suit the publisher. A name is everything, it sells the book, and since the little pseudonym had *had a good run*, we basically wanted to keep it. When Delatouche was asked, he settled the matter with a compromise: Sand would stay the same, and I'd take another first name just for myself. Without giving it much thought, I seized upon the name of George, which seemed to me synonymous with the Berry. Jules and George, unknown to the public, would pass for brothers and cousins.[12]

And so Aurore Dudevant became "George Sand" in literature. Everything was decided in just minutes, if one can believe what she says. Still disguised as a *man* of letters, she only had to choose a masculine first name. For her, literature was definitely a thing to be shared among friends and comrades; she was making her dreams come true among lads from Berry now living in Paris, childhood friends and cousins, George, Jules, Henri, and a few others. For "George Sand," it seemed just one more step toward autonomy and a steady income; in fact, the very enthusiastic reception given to *Indiana* was going to thrust the author to the forefront of the literary scene of Paris.

In all respects, there is nothing banal about the publication of *Indiana* or the choice of the pseudonym on its cover. For starters, literary pseudonyms were much less frequent than is often said. For a long time women authors, quite like men authors and for the same reasons, had been doing all kinds of things to get into print, from publishing their works anonymously or under their real names or husband's name if they were married. Most nineteenth-century women authors who were George Sand's contemporaries, such as Flora Tristan, Delphine de Girardin, Hortense Allart, or Marceline Desbordes-Valmore, published under their own names, except in newspapers where a generally masculine "pen name" was the usual practice. Marie d'Agoult alone chose to imitate Sand when she signed her books as "Daniel Stern." What authors built a literary career around an invented name of their own choosing? What authors little by little took on the literary identity they had chosen for themselves? Very few, in fact. Voltaire in the eighteenth century, and in the nineteenth, just Stendhal and Gérard de Nerval (who kept his first name), and later Lautréamont (Isidore Ducasse) and Rachilde (Marguerite Eymery) chose a pseudonym and "became" the character they had created in their books.

Yet the matter of the (false) name was not entirely settled thanks to a few quick words with Delatouche, as George Sand maintains in her autobiography. *Indiana* is signed "G. Sand," like her second novel *Valentine*, published in November 1832. When she signed with the full first name, Sand first used the French form "Georges." Several short stories that appeared in newspapers between the fall of 1832 and the spring of 1833 were also signed with the name "Georges Sand." When *Lelia* was published in July 1833, more than a year after *Indiana*, "George Sand" appeared for the first time on the book's cover in its definitive spelling. Furthermore, in March 1832 Aurore Dudevant began using the initial G. in her private correspondence, instead of her usual A.

G.? Sand could have chosen that letter in memory of the young Irish girl she met at the convent of English Augustinian Sisters in 1818. As Sand herself wrote, the behavior of this mischievous eleven-year-old designated as "Mary G***" in *Story of My Life* created quite a sensation among the young boarding students. Since Mary Gillibrand "was not a member of our sex by temperament,"[13] she was nicknamed *boy*. The use of the initial G. probably owes something to the "tomboy" who made such an impression on Aurore and whose family name also started with the same letter.

George? In Berrichon folklore there is an impish devil known as "Georgeon," and Sand reports his pranks in her *Country Legends* [*Légendes rustiques*]. But there is no Berrichon peasant with this first name in either the novels or the open letters about rural conditions that Sand briefly signed with the fictive name Blaise Bonnin. On the other hand, George is Byron's first name, a European idol since his tragic death at Missolonghi in 1824. Sand would remember his epic poems, *Lara* and *The Corsair*, in her first novels. George is also the first name of the last two kings of England, George III and George IV, who succeeded his father in 1820.

Sand? The word exists in English (but not as an English family name), and no doubt when Delatouche thought it up, he was thinking of exploiting the popularity of novels translated from that language. Yet Sand, as everybody knew at the time, was also the name of an assassin, Karl-Ludwig Sand. In 1820 he stabbed the German playwright August von Kotzebue, suspected of being a Russian agent, and was executed a short time later. In *Story of My Life* Sand denies being in favor of "political assassination."[14] Still she recalls that the choice of the name "Sand" did a lot for her reputation in Germany.[15]

So the pseudonym "George Sand" looks like a puff pastry layered with odd bits of history and legend, mixing together the Berry region, Germany, and England, with a number of exclusively masculine celebrities thrown in for good measure. When she adopted this name, choosing not only to sign her works with it but also to use it in her daily life and to become a purely imagined other person, Aurore Dudevant performed a true revolution for herself, a revolution that had probably started much earlier, as will be seen later on. She shook up the cues of gender, yielded to the urge to engender herself, abolishing the notion of the *family* name and everything related to history, inheritance, affiliation, that it connotes. Thanks to the pseudonym, "the individual named G[eorge] Sand"[16] is no longer anybody's daughter or wife; she becomes the son/daughter of her works. "In Paris," she wrote to her friend Laure Decerfz on 7 July 1832, "Madame Dudevant is dead. But George Sand is known as a hale and hearty fellow."[17]

Some twenty years later, having once and for all *become* "George Sand," she observed in *Story of My Life*: "What is a name in our revolutionized and revolutionary world? A number for those who are doing nothing, a sign or a slogan for those who are working and fighting. The one I've been given, I made it all by myself and all alone after the fact, by my own work. . . . I live, from day to day, on this name that protects my work. . . . My tranquil conscience doesn't think anything needs to be changed about the name designating and personifying it."[18]

I

1804–1831

"IN MUSIC AND ROSY PINK"

"On day twelve of Messidor in year twelve of the Republic,"[1] meaning 1 July 1804, a little girl was born in Paris, at 15 rue Meslée (in what is now the fifth arrondissement). The name on her birth certificate read Amantine-Aurore-Lucile Dupin. Sand recalled in *Story of My Life*: "That day mother was wearing a pretty rose-pink dress, and my father was playing a contredanse of his own invention on his faithful violin from Cremona . . . ; my mother felt a bit ill, left the dance and went to her room. . . . At the end of the dance my aunt Lucie went into my mother's room and promptly exclaimed, 'Come here, Maurice, you've got a daughter.' 'I'll name her Aurore, for my poor mother who is not here to bless her, but some day the little one will have her blessing,' said my father taking me in his arms. . . . 'She was born in music and rosy pink; she'll have a happy life,' said my aunt."[2] What a charming picture, with Aunt Lucie acting like a good fairy and predicting a fine future for the child. But upon closer inspection, the present and past were much less rosy than the future mother's dress might suggest, and the same goes for what would follow. This birth in music in fact masks many problems and goes along with a few unsolved mysteries.

Aurore's parents brought together two worlds dead set against each other, both then and in later years: a twenty-six year-old army officer, a "terribly spoiled"[3] son, and a woman five years his senior from a very humble background. On the paternal side of the family, there was a king and one of the greatest military strategists of the eighteenth century, Maurice de Saxe; on the maternal side, a bird-seller, a cart-driver, and a scrap-iron seller whose names are not even known.[4] "In my veins the blood of kings mixed with the blood of the poor and the powerless,"[5] declared the author of *Story of My Life*, conscious of the enormous contrasts in her family history. These may get less attention than the illegitimate children present in every generation, including her own.

Maurice Dupin and Sophie-Victoire Delaborde were married the month before their daughter was born, thereby legalizing a union begun in Italy in late 1800. Together they had already had at least two children, a son in 1801 and a daughter in 1803. Their names are not known, and both died in infancy. The young man's mother, Marie-Aurore Dupin, was worried about her son's affair with a woman of questionable morals. To be sure, her only son was very considerate and wrote to her regularly ever since leaving her house for a career in the Army of the Republic. Yet he kept hidden from her a relationship that she promptly divined, and for years she tried in vain to break it off.

Born in 1748, Marie-Aurore Dupin was the illegitimate daughter of Maurice de Saxe, himself the illegitimate son of Frederick-Augustus, elector of Saxony and future king of Poland, and his mistress, Maria-Aurora von Kœnigsmarck. Having become the marshal general of the King's Camps and Armies, the victor in the Battle of Fontenoy counted among his conquests a young actress by the name of Marie Rainteau, who, more for gallantry than for theater, took the name of Mlle de Verrière. She saw to it that the daughter born of her months-long affair with the great soldier was recognized and lined up high-placed protection for Marie-Aurore: at the Convent of Saint-Cyr, her daughter received an education befitting a young lady of the best society. After a first marriage, short and stormy, Marie-Aurore, age twenty-nine, was wed to Louis-Claude Dupin de Francueil, age sixty-one. She seems to have spent happy years with this wealthy man who was a friend to the Enlightenment. For a short time Jean-Jacques Rousseau, who would dedicate a few pages to him in his *Confessions*, was Dupin de Francueil's guest and secretary.

Widowed in 1786, Marie-Aurore Dupin first continued to live in the imposing Raoul château in Châteauroux. In 1793 she bought an estate at Nohant that better suited her income, greatly reduced after the Revolution. Six years later, in 1799, her son, the young captain Maurice Dupin, fathered a son he refused to recognize. This child was registered under the name of Pierre Laverdure, but he seems to have born the name of his mother, Chatiron. Upon the child's birth, Mlle Chatiron, a laundress at the château of Nohant, was invited to come live in a little house nearby. Maurice seems not to have shown much interest in any of this. His mother, on the other hand, looked after "the child from the *little house*,"[6] as he was generally known. Although Hippolyte was reared with Aurore, it took her years to understand just how she was related to her half brother.

As for Sand's mother, Sophie-Victoire Delaborde, born in Paris in 1773, was the daughter of one of the bird-sellers who traditionally did business alongside seed merchants and herbalists on the quai of the Seine near the Conciergerie. "Orphaned and hungry at the age of fourteen,"[7] she was probably reduced to prostitution. Bearing her first child at seventeen, she had several children of unknown paternity, including a daughter, Caroline Delaborde, born in 1799, before her departure for Italy with Adjutant Collin who was stationed there. In Italy she met another officer, Maurice Dupin, became his mistress, and then openly started living with him.

Did she continue her loose living? Wasn't she often separated from her lover because his regiment was moving around? True, she spent the year before Aurore's birth in Paris; her friend Pierret, who did odd jobs for her, rarely left her side and remained attached to her his whole life long.[8] Meanwhile Maurice was posted in the north, in Charleville and then Sedan, all the while enjoying regular leaves with his wife in Paris.

While she was writing *Story of My Life* and trying to organize her father's correspondence, Sand seems to have briefly doubted her own legitimacy.[9] Hadn't her grandmother made damning revelations about her mother, and hadn't Sand been unable to get to the bottom of them? Hardly inclined to praise her daughter-in-law's virtues, had Mme Dupin been repeating nasty gossip? Were her suspicions groundless? No evidence can prove or disprove the doubts that besieged Sand. Writing *Story of My Life*, she arranged certain facts and probably ignored others. As to the place and date of her birth, she had also heard all kinds of contradictory tales and said that her birthday was always celebrated on 5 July, not the 1st.

Now married and father to a son and a little girl, Maurice went on saying nothing about his private life in his letters to his mother. She grew worried and finally asked the mayor of the fifth arrondissement to check out "the person with whom he [Maurice] had contracted marriage." She added: "Since he's been living in rue Meslay [Meslée], my son has had a daughter that I believe was born in Messidor [July]."[10] An answer arrived, confirming the mother's suspicions. For a moment she considered having the marriage annulled, then abandoned the idea. Some weeks later, Maurice presented the little girl to Mme Dupin on a visit to Paris. As in a Greuze painting or one of those melodramas then in vogue in the theaters, the old lady wept tenderly at the sight of her granddaughter and forgave her son. So now young Aurore was "adopted" by her grandmother and, from the looks of it, legitimized in all respects.

She spent her first years in Paris in humble apartments, first in rue Meslée, then boulevard Poissonnière, and finally rue Grange-Batelière, the site of her first memories:

> I remember perfectly the apartment where we lived in rue Grange-Batelière. . . . That's where the precise and nearly continuous stream of my memory got started. . . . I have just a hazy memory of long hours that I spent lying awake in my little bed and busily contemplating some fold in the curtain or flower in the wallpaper. . . .
>
> . . . I walked at ten months, started talking rather late, but once I had said a few words, I learned them all very fast, and at the age of four I could read really well. We were also taught to pray, and I remember reciting my prayers from one end to the other without batting an eye or understanding a single thing.[11]

While Aurore was spending quiet days with her mother, her half sister, Caroline, and faithful Pierret (the only memorable event was "seeing the King of Rome in the arms of his nurse"[12]), her father, "often away,"[13] was following Napoleon's armies around France and Europe, writing frequent letters to his mother and his wife.

Although Sand partially rewrote and embellished these letters in her autobiography, adding, for example, literary quotations and expurgating a romantic episode,[14] they give a very lively chronicle of military life during the Consulate and the Napoleonic Empire, with an abundance of evocative details and personal impressions. First a captain and then a major in the First Regiment of Hussards, Maurice Dupin participated in the Bavarian, Prussian, and Polish campaigns. In early 1808 he left for Spain as an aide-de-camp for Prince Murat, chosen by the emperor to direct the maneuvers of the thousands of soldiers sent down there. Maurice Dupin would only stay a few months in that country ravaged by a particularly villainous and deadly war of conquest that Francisco Goya immortalized in his painting *Tres de mayo* and his engravings *Desastres de la guerra*, which Sand would evoke in the prologue of *The Devil's Pool* [*La mare au diable*].

In April Sophie Dupin, pregnant once again, decided to go join her husband in Madrid. Sand would retain particularly vivid memories of this trip to Spain, a brief stay in Madrid while her mother gave birth to a son, the family's return trip through a famine-stricken country, dedicating two chapters of *Story of My Life* to them. She remembered staying with her parents in the royal palace requisitioned by Murat, who had just turned Carlos IV and his family out of these quarters. Her father had a little aide-de-camp's uniform made for her, and she paraded it in front of Murat. Soon she had "the most beautiful toys in the world"[15] (which the king's children had just abandoned) and saw herself in a full-size mirror for the first time. She found her mother, dressed in a Spanish costume, a black silk dress with a fringe and a black mantilla, "surprisingly beautiful."[16]

A boy named Louis, blind and particularly puny, was born on 12 June 1808. (Sand had witnessed the birth, in 1805, of another little boy who lived but a few months.) When the child was just two weeks old, Maurice Dupin and his family decided to leave "Spain in flames"[17] and go back to Nohant. From Madrid, Maurice Dupin wrote to his mother: "I'm saving my newborn son's baptism for a celebration in Nohant. What a fine opportunity to ring the bells and have a village ball!"[18] The grueling trip back took several weeks. The two children came down with fevers; on the way they caught scabies, which was treated by mixing sulfur into their food. At Nohant, where she arrived for the first time in her life on 21 July 1808, Aurore met her half brother Hippolyte as well as her father's old tutor, Jean-Louis-François Deschartres, and renewed acquaintance with her grandmother, a small woman with a commanding presence. She was wearing a brown silk dress, a "blond wig with a frizzy tuft over the forehead," and a "little round hat with a lace cockade in the middle."[19]

Finally Maurice seemed to have the "total happiness"[20] he'd been dreaming about for the last eight years. His wife and two children, Aurore and Louis, were now with him in Nohant. His mother, who had not stopped quaking since he had gone to war, finally felt reassured, even though she had desired a better match for her son. Tragedy would strike a few weeks later: "On Friday 8 September the poor little blind baby, after whimpering a long time on my mother's knees, went cold, and nothing could warm him up. Deschartres came and took him from my mother's arms. He was dead."[21] Crazed with grief, Sophie Dupin had the newborn buried, then dug him up so that she could spend a full day beside the corpse to make sure the baby was really dead. Then she laid him to rest in the garden, at the foot of a pear tree, and started gardening on his improvised grave with Aurore and Hippolyte.

From Spain Maurice Dupin had brought back a horse named Leopardo, a gift from Murat. He was a wonderful horse, but terribly skittish, and his master did not trust him—for good reason:

On Friday 17 September, he mounted his terrifying horse to go visit our friends in La Châtre. He had dinner there and spent the evening. . . . Just outside of town, a hundred feet beyond the bridge that marks the entrance, the road makes a turn. . . . My father had started galloping after the bridge. He was riding the fateful Leopardo. . . . At the bend in the road my father's horse ran into a pile of rocks in the dark. He did not come crashing down, but . . . he reared up so violently that the rider was thrown off and fell ten feet backward. Weber . . . found his master lying on his back, without any apparent wounds; but he had broken the vertebrae in his neck and was already dead.[22]

There is no way to describe the shock and grief at the announce-ment of Maurice's death. Marie-Aurore Dupin went on foot from Nohant to the spot where her son fell and threw herself down on his body. Deschartres laughed convulsively before bursting into tears: "My mother fell into a chair behind the bed. I can see her livid face, her long dark hair floating on her chest, her bare arms that I kept kissing; I can hear her heartrending shrieks. . . . The pain and horror of it all demolished me, annihilating my sense of what was going on."[23] The house and the village of Nohant were plunged into a turmoil of grief. Superstitious servants claimed to see Maurice walking around the house in his dress uniform. He was buried as close as possible to his family, "in a little vault under the cemetery wall so that his head lay at rest in the garden and his feet in hallowed ground."[24]

Eager to entertain her granddaughter, Marie-Aurore Dupin found her a playmate, a maidservant's daughter, Ursule. She was dressed in full mourning like Aurore and stayed at the château (some years later she would leave Nohant to become an appren-tice). Marie-Aurore's plans were soon drawn up. She did not want her daughter-in-law staying on at Nohant any longer, but she had grown terribly attached to Aurore, who had become a substi-tute for her son Maurice, dead at the age of thirty-one. As Sand remembers in *Story of My Life*, "My voice, my features, my man-ners, my tastes, everything about me, reminded her so much of her son as a child that sometimes, as she was watching me play, she would entertain a sort of illusion, often calling me Maurice and referring to me as *her son*. . . . I also showed musical talent . . . and she found that charming because it reminded her of my father's childhood, and she became a young mother once again by giving me lessons."[25]

The little girl quickly guessed what was afoot and got terribly worried. She found herself torn between her "passionate love" for her mother—begging her not to "*give her up for money*"[26] to her grandmother—and her affection for a levelheaded, well-educated, and extremely courteous woman. In comparison with the great lady, the young plebeian seemed all the more bad mannered, ill tempered, and poorly educated. The plans for separation were more and more detailed, guaranteeing a comfortable life for Aurore as well as a proper education for a gentleman's daughter. Everybody was getting involved, and Aurore was distraught. "Do you want to go back to eating beans in your little garret room?"[27] one of the maids asked the little girl.

On 3 February 1809, five months after her son's death, Marie-Aurore Dupin made a legal commitment to pay 1,500 *livres tournois* per year to Sophie-Victoire Delaborde, who, in return, agreed that her mother-in-law would have legal custody of her daughter. For a long time Aurore would have the feeling that her grandmother had bought her from her mother and that an old, grief-stricken woman with aristocratic obsessions had separated her from the person she loved most of all. A victory of power and money over weakness and poverty? Aurore thought so for a good many years, but she was wrong. Her mother was not unhappy about an arrangement to which she had readily agreed, one that guaranteed her a small income and freed her from working.

All the same, once this contract was signed, Aurore Dupin's family assumed a strange and unusual structure. Maurice Dupin was dead, and his wife went back to Paris with her daughter Caroline. That meant that Aurore had lost both parents. After 1809 she would only see Sophie Dupin intermittently, a few days in Paris in the winter, a few weeks in Nohant during the summer. Her sixty-five-year-old grandmother served as a mother to the girl of five. Deschartres became her tutor, doctor, and moral guide;

Hippolyte was reared alongside her. The reconstituted family included two adults and two children (in the beginning, there were four, with two born outside of wedlock), plus Ursule. The two adults were not together for reasons of heart, one being the employee of the other, and the half brother was never more than an illegitimate child being raised alongside a legitimate one, Maurice's sole "remnant." Curiously enough, Marie-Aurore Dupin did not rediscover Maurice's character and features in the son he had had with a laundress, but in the daughter of a woman with a shady past who had become her daughter-in-law in 1804. It was her grand-daughter, perhaps because she was just barely legitimate, that she decided to treat as her son, the heir to her name and fortune.

Symbolically, Aurore took the place of her dead father, and she was always supposed to be a reminder of his existence. This peculiar script gave her two genders, her own as well as the one her grandmother authorized when she called the girl Maurice and acknowledged her as her son: "You look too much like your father," she said one day seeing the girl in trousers, prepared to go horseback riding. "There are moments when I get the past and the present so mixed up that I no longer know where I am in my life."[28] This resemblance that made her both boy and girl, Aurore and Maurice, haunts *Story of My Life*. Much later, when she chose George as her pen name, Aurore may have been reenacting something that had left a deep mark on her life as a little girl.

Sand's only novel with the word "family" in the title came out in 1861: *The Family Germandre* [*La famille de Germandre*], now forgotten. In this book the novelist shakes up some preconceived ideas about the name, legacy, and connections that a family of minor Berrichon aristocrats seem to take as their birthright. She tells the story of several generations of the family and imagines them happily all together in the final pages. The novel is set in 1808, a key moment in her own story, since the family then seemed to have achieved "complete happiness" for a moment. This is the only one of Sand's novels to take place at that time, as if the mere mention of the word "family" were enough to make personal experience come flooding back all of a sudden and to conjure up from these memories their fantastic double, the well-spring of the novel.

GROWING UP IN NOHANT

Aside from short visits to Paris where she stayed with her grandmother in an elegant apartment in rue Neuve-des-Mathurins, Aurore spent the next nine years at Nohant. This period began with the signing of the contract between Marie-Aurore Dupin and her daughter-in-law and ended with Aurore's being sent to Paris, to the convent of English Augustinian Sisters, to complete her education.

After the trip to Madrid cut short Aurore Dupin's early years in Paris, the most significant moments of her childhood mainly took place in a little village in Berry. Quite isolated from the rest of the countryside because the roads were hardly passable except in summer, the Black Valley [Vallée-Noire], "a huge valley measuring some 120 square miles . . . , with the villages of Marche and Bourbonnais on its southern edge,"[29] has a few villages (Ardentes, Château-Meillant, Briantes, Sainte-Sévère, Sarzay, Nohant, Saint-Chartier), some isolated farms, and even a desolate moor called Brande where travelers often went astray—Aurore, her mother and a maid got lost there one memorable evening on their way back to Nohant. "The Black Valley," as Sand recalled in the preface of her novel *Valentine*, "was me, it was the setting, the trappings of my existence."[30]

The estate that Marie-Aurore Dupin bought in Nohant in 1793 consisted of a well-proportioned manor with outbuildings, 240 hectares of woods and farmland as well as three farms with the names Launières, Porte, and Chicoterie.[31] It was considered one of the great landed estates of the department of the Indre. Mme Dupin lived on a relatively modest income from her properties, in addition to rents from a building in Paris and a few securities.

Built in 1767 by Pierre Péarron de Serennes on the foundation of an old fortified castle, the manor has a front courtyard. The trees growing there now were planted by Sand in 1844, and the courtyard is enclosed by a gate with a little lodge on either side. There are outbuildings on the left, to the right a farmhouse with a stable. A second courtyard is located further to the right, one side of which is a huge barn.[32]

The design of the house is in keeping with the architecture of the second half of the eighteenth century. On the ground floor there is a huge vestibule flanked by a majestic stairway with a wooden banister. Mme Dupin put in the stairs when she bought the property. The vestibule leads to the formal area that looks out on the garden, a large dining room followed by a parlor decorated with paintings. To the left are Mme Dupin's rooms, her bedroom, where she entertained her friends and acquaintances, played music, and took her meals when alone, plus a boudoir and a dressing room. Aurore slept on the second floor in one of the four big rooms with a view of the garden. Deschartres occupied a little room with a view of the courtyard, to the left of the stairs. The servants had their rooms on the third floor, with their own stairs. The garden, with a vegetable patch and an orchard, was redesigned by Mme Dupin. She rarely set foot in it, maintaining prerevolutionary habits, just taking a few steps in silk slippers while leaning on a servant's arm.

Mme Dupin was friends with most of the local château owners, wealthy members of the bourgeoisie of Châteauroux, La Châtre, and nearby villages. Their children would become her grand-daughter's friends, particularly after she was married, and Aurore would get together with some of them again in Paris. Charles Duvernet's family lived in the château of Coudray, and the family of Gustave Papet in the château of Ars; Adolphe Duplomb, Alexis Duteil, Alphonse Fleury, Jules Néraud, Ernest Périgois, Gabriel Planet, and François Rollinat, most of whom became lawyers, would be her lifelong friends.

Living in Nohant with an elderly lady educated at the Convent of Saint-Cyr more than half a century earlier was soon trouble. Mme Dupin had scarcely got rid of her daughter-in-law when she told her granddaughter to change her tone and manners, to stop saying *tu* to the servants so that they would not be tempted to reply in kind, to address her in the third person as much as possible ("Will my dear grandmother allow me to go to the garden?"[33]). "Rolling on the ground, laughing uproariously, speaking Berrichon dialect,"[34] such things were no longer permitted. Mme Dupin recommended *retenue* or restraint in all things, mastering one's words and actions; she imposed her calm, orderly habits on a little girl of five who dreamed of nothing but running and skipping around: "I felt she was closing me up with her in a big box when she would tell me: 'Go play quietly.' She would give me prints to look at, and I didn't see them, my head was spinning. A dog barking outside, a bird singing in the garden would give me a start. I would have liked to be the dog or the bird."[35] For Aurore, her "little mother's passionate hugs"[36] were followed by the rather chilly and solemn kisses of an old lady altogether eager to set an example and triumph over her young granddaughter's "capricious and unmanageable"[37] disposition. Mme Dupin saw in this behavior the influence of a mother of meager intelligence and virtue.

Marie-Aurore Dupin undertook the mission of seeing that Maurice's daughter and her eventual heir would have good manners as well as a solid education. She would teach Aurore music all alone,[38] but for everything else, her granddaughter would be entrusted to the man who had tutored her father.

Deschartres was an amazing character! One of the major figures in Mme Dupin's life—aside from servants, he was the only man who lived under her roof after her husband's death in 1786, when she was still residing in Châteauroux—he also played a central role in the life of her son Maurice, who lost his father as an adolescent, and then in Aurore's life as well. As a young man, he quit his job as a professor at the Cardinal Lemoine School in Paris after he had been hired as the Dupin family's private tutor. Deschartres was not only a learned man, of humble origins, who found in wealthy aristocratic households a way of life that gave him a certain degree of liberty and material comfort. He was also Mme Dupin's secretary once she had lost her husband, her business manager and adviser.

In addition, he took great interest in economics, trying, apparently without much success, to boost the production of Nohant's farm-lands and a little terrain of his own. Keenly interested in medicine as well, he introduced Aurore to dissection and sometimes took her to visit his patients, Berrichon peasants whom he treated for free. Curious about everything, taking correspondence courses in "physics, chemistry, medicine, and surgery,"[39] he also knew a fair amount about astronomy and botany. A materialist through and through, he would have long conversations with his adolescent pupil about religion and the meaning of life.

When Mme Dupin bought Nohant, Deschartres was thirty-two years old. He was forty-seven and the mayor of Nohant when Maurice Dupin returned from Spain with his family in July 1808. This erudite man, with all kinds of qualities, and one great flaw—intolerable vanity—never married and seems not to have had any kind of attachment:

> He had never been in a religious order. Even so, he could not rid himself of a nickname I had attached to his all-encompassing competence and self-important air; from then on nobody ever called him anything but *the great man*.
>
> He had been handsome as a lad, and he still was when my grandmother took him on: neat and tidy, clean-shaven, with a sparkle in his eye, and prominent calf muscles. In short, he really looked like a tutor. But I am sure nobody . . . could have ever looked at him without a laugh, given that the word *pedant* was clearly written on every line in his face and every move he made.
>
> . . . He was tremendously knowledgeable, very abstemious, and madly courageous. He possessed every fine quality of soul, along with an insufferable disposition and a degree of smugness close to delirium. . . . But what devotion, what zeal, what a generous and sensitive soul![40]

Deschartres left the house after Mme Dupin died, in the wake of a financial disagreement with Aurore's mother. His pupil who would soon marry and bear a son still saw him occasionally in Paris up until his death in the spring of 1828. Sometimes she wondered if he had killed himself. Deschartres took with him "a considerable portion" of Aurore Dupin's life, "all my childhood memories, happy and sad, all the stimulus, sometimes irritating, sometimes beneficial, of my intellectual development."[41] He also left the mystery of his character and the reasons for his behavior, about which the autobiographer may have chosen to keep silent.

Maurice Dupin had been a lazy and extremely spoiled pupil. Deschartres had tried his best to follow his charge's progress in the areas that he was unable to teach him—German, music, fencing—and for which other instructors had been hired. In 1793, when Mme Dupin had just been arrested by the revolutionary Committee of Public Safety [Comité de salut public], he was told to burn a good part of her papers so that nothing could be held against her. A second installment in his life as a tutor began in 1809. This time he was put in charge of teaching Aurore, her half brother Hippolyte, and Ursule, the little servant-girl being reared at the château. The two little girls were rather docile, but Hippolyte's mischievous pranks and "naughty pleasures"[42] were too numerous to be counted: "One day he threw burning logs into the fireplace, saying he was *sacrificing to the gods of the underworld*, and he set the house on fire. Another day he packed a huge log with gunpowder so that it would explode and blow pot roast all over the kitchen. He called that studying volcanic theory. And then he attached a saucepan to the dogs' tails. . . . He gave the cats wooden shoes, meaning he glued nutshells to their four paws and threw them down on the ice or parquet floors."[43] Hippolyte was often "cruelly thrashed" by his short-tempered tutor. To the two little girls the "great man" only "said silly things."[44] *Story of My Life* doesn't exactly say what the grandmother, who treated Maurice's two children in ways so similar and so different at one and the same time, thought about this.

Several years went by. Deschartres's pupil began to find his lessons more and more tedious:

> Deschartres was giving me a Latin lesson that I was taking less
> and less well, for this dead language didn't interest me one bit;

and a lesson in French prosody left me nauseated, since this came to me no more naturally than arithmetic at which I've always been notoriously bad. . . . For me, botany was nothing more than a bunch of purely arbitrary classifications . . . plus Greek and Latin nomenclature just a dry chore of memorization. . . . I wondered, in my superb ignorance, what was the use of all these alignments and withering rules that hampered flights of thought and froze it in place.[45]

Such an education, at first sight rather catch-as-catch-can, was in keeping with a time that had not yet established a national school-system. Only after the Guizot law of 1833 was a system of elementary schools set up all over France. In these last years of the Empire, boys from wealthy families were generally sent to Catholic boarding schools and then went on to some form of higher education or a military academy, as was the case for Hippolyte. Girls would spend a few years in a convent, where intellectual aspirations were sometimes very limited.

Outside of these schools, which varied greatly in form and quality, homeschooling was the general rule, in the city as well as the countryside. Peasants usually got some education only through the catechism classes that prepared them for communion.[46] An apprentice, a house-servant, or even a servant's child might happen upon a master or mistress who would teach them to read and write. This was the case for Ursule, reared alongside Aurore on her grandmother's recommendation, and also a peasant child named Liset whom Sophie Dupin and then Aurore Dupin briefly looked after.[47] As a rule, the literacy rate remained low out in the country, and education, often left to chance, was minimal—in 1850 only about 50 percent of boys were in school.

Aurore hardly seemed convinced of the need for education or, at least, for the knowledge the imperious Deschartres threw at her. She rejected it in the name of the resolutely "romantic"[48] side of her character. The epithet often resurfaces in *Story of My Life*. For Sand, the word designated one of the specific traits of her "nature"—constantly thwarted, curbed, hectored by the people around her—and voiced a resolute plea: to be what she wanted, whenever and however she wanted it. The incessant dream of an elsewhere corresponding to her desires and needs, the constant wish for a transformed reality, the great longing for fiction, come up again and again in her narration of these years in Berry. In later years George Sand would tell Henriette La Bigottière that she was a "born novelist,"[49] marrying masculine and feminine traits and never hesitating to make "storytelling" one of her innate qualities.

Fortunately, growing up in Nohant meant something besides the limits determined by a grandmother obsessed with fine manners and Deschartres's somewhat iron-fisted, ragtag schooling. Just outside the château there beckoned the countryside and the seasonal rhythms of the peasants' work, their rustic language, habits, and ways of life, plus the many children to run around with and "just act like a kid":[50]

> I knew where to go find Fanchon, Pierrot, Liline, Rosette, or Sylvain, in what field, pasture, or road. We would wreak *havoc* in the ditches, trees, and streams. We would shepherd our flocks, meaning not shepherding them at all, and while the goats and sheep were grazing on the green wheat to their hearts' content, we would dance wildly or picnic in the grass on our flat cakes, cheese, and dark bread. We would go right ahead and milk the goats and the ewes, even the cows and the mares when they weren't too recalcitrant. We would roast birds and potatoes in the embers. Pears and wild apples, blackthorn berries, blackberries, roots, everything was a feast for us. . . . Every season had its pleasures. While the hay was being taken in, what fun it was rolling around way up high on the loaded carts or the little stacks.[51]
>
> . . . Fall and winter were the most fun. Children in the country are freer and less busy. Before the wheat headed up in March, there were huge fields where the herds could wander without doing any harm. So the animals looked after themselves while the shepherds gathered around their wind-blown fires, talking, playing, dancing, or telling stories.[52]

> . . . During the winter my grandmother let me entertain my
> *social circle* in the big dining room that was well heated by an
> old stove. My social circle was twenty-some children from the
> township who brought in their *saulnées*, which are immensely
> long strings fitted out with all kinds of horsehair slipknots for
> snaring larks and other small field birds when there's snow on the
> ground. . . . We would set the snares out before dawn in all the
> right places. After sweeping the snow away all along the furrow,
> we would throw down grain, and two hours later we would find
> hundreds of larks in the snares. The donkey would bring back
> huge sacks filled with our harvest.[53]

Lots of details in *Story of My Life* about life in the Berry countryside resurface in the rustic novels, starting with *La petite fadette*,
written at the same time as the passages just quoted from Sand's
autobiography. It is easy to understand how much these activities
counted in the life of a little girl very often left to her own devices,
her indestructible attachment to Berry and the world of peasants
being a direct result. Whenever possible, especially when family
tensions became too great, Aurore would run out into the fields
and drown her sorrows with "the kids that liked me and rescued
me from my solitude . . . tearing around over the roads, bushes,
and pastures more than ever."[54]

Her connection with Hippolyte, "more and more unruly,"[55]
became gradually more distant. The two adolescents no longer
shared the same games, and Aurore's somewhat forced levity often
turned to "sulkiness and then tears."[56] Plus, Hippolyte would soon
join the army, following in his father's footsteps. Mme Dupin's
health required more and more care. She spent most of her time
in her room, taking long naps and giving her granddaughter a few
minutes every two or three days for a brief harpsichord lesson.
Aurore got bored, and this reawakened the pain of separation from
Sophie Dupin. There continued profound strife between Maurice's
mother and her daughter-in-law, and Aurore suffered terribly from
the enmity of the women whom she, unable to choose either one
or the other, called "my two mothers."[57] Years later Sand would

sum things up in these terms: "Placed in an strange situation between these two loves, . . . I was by turns made victim of these two women's feelings, and of my own, which they did nothing to spare,"[58] and "my mother and my grandmother, both avid for my love, ripped my heart to shreds."[59]

The first letters we have of Aurore date from this time. In 1812, at the age of eight, she wrote to her mother on stationery with little designs in the margins:

> How sad not to be able to say goodbye to you! You see how sad
> it makes me to leave you. Goodbye, keep me in your thoughts,
> and be sure I won't forget you.
>
> Your daughter[60]

Three years later, during the winter of 1815, she wrote to reassure her mother:

> Oh! yes, dear mother, I kiss you, I'm waiting for you, I want
> you and I'm dying of impatience to see you here [in Nohant].
> My God! how you worry about me! Stop worrying, dear little
> mother. I'm just fine. I'm taking advantage of the beautiful
> weather, walking, running, coming and going, having fun. I'm
> eating well, I'm sleeping even better and think about you even
> more.
>
> Goodbye, dear mother, so don't worry one bit. I kiss you with
> all my heart.
>
> Aurore[61]

Her desire to go back and live in Paris with her mother and half sister, Caroline, grew stronger every day. Aurore must have been twelve or thirteen when she openly rebelled against her grand-mother and the education she was getting. One day she stated loud and clear that she wanted to be sent away from Nohant. Having heard about this from her chambermaid, the grandmother decided to come down hard on such a display of ingratitude. Aurore was confined to her room and given nothing but dry bread. Another maid intervened, and the grandmother soon agreed to talk with the girl.

Hoping to make her granddaughter finally understand the reasons for her own behavior, Marie-Aurore Dupin decided to pull out all the stops and give Aurore certain details about her mother to which the girl had not been made privy. She went down on her knees begging Aurore to listen to what she had to say, without sparing her a single particular:

> It would have been possible to reveal this awful story without destroying my respect and love for my mother. . . . It was enough to tell me everything, the reasons for her misfortunes, isolation and poverty starting at the age of fourteen, the corruption of rich men who lie in wait for hunger and innocence, the merciless rigor of opinion allowing no way back and no means of atonement. . . . I was made to understand that while I was being told everything about the past, the present was being spared me, and that there was some new secret in my mother's life that nobody wanted to tell me, something that would make me tremble for my own future if I insisted on living with her. . . . My mother was a lost woman, and I a blind child who wanted to throw herself into an abyss.[62]

These revelations had a dreadful effect on Aurore. There were no words for her suffering. She hated her mother, hated herself, and had no desire for anything. One minute she was utterly dejected, and the next giddy with excitement. Her behavior was quite mad. Seeing Aurore's extravagant ways, her grandmother decided to pack her off to the convent. Much to everyone's surprise, her mother, despite her prejudices against her mother-in-law's ideas, thought this an excellent notion. Aurore had no choice but to obey:

> —So be it, I thought to myself; I don't know what a convent is, but it'll be something new; and after all, since I'm having no fun at all in this life of mine, the change will do me good.
>
> . . . I felt an imperative need to have a rest from all these heartrending conflicts; I was tired of being an apple of discord

between two people I loved. I would almost have preferred to be forgotten.[63]

On 12 January 1818 Aurore Dupin and her grandmother crossed the threshold of the convent of English Augustinian Sisters located near the Pantheon. This convent and the main street nearby, the rue des Fossés-Saint-Victor, disappeared when the rue Cardinal-Lemoine was opened up, but the Scottish and Irish convents are still there.

Along with Sacré-Cœur and the Abbaye-aux-Bois, this religious institution of English origin was then one of three fashionable convents for the schooling of upper-class young ladies. While the sisters and a good number of the pupils were English, the Mortemart, Chabot, Greffulhe, Montmorency, and La Rochejacquelein families sent their daughters there. Classes were given in French and English by teachers recruited in France and living at the convent, the sisters reserving for themselves the teaching of catechism. Some teaching was done in the convent parlor, the teacher on one side of the grille, and pupil on the other: "Everything was in English there, the past and present, and once you had gone beyond the grille, you felt as though you were on the other side of the English Channel. I was a peasant girl from Berry, and this amazed me, made my head spin for a full week."[64]

Built around a huge garden with trees and a vegetable patch, the vast complex was directed at that time by an Englishwoman of the best society, the Reverend Mother Mrs. Canning, who was endowed with "an astute mind."[65] Aurore would spend two years in this cloistered space whose street-side windows were covered with grilles and canvas. There was no contact with the outside world aside from visits in the convent parlor and exceptional outings. More than a hundred women lived in the convent then, "ordained nuns . . . , lay sisters, boarding students, lodgers, secular teachers, and servants."[66] For the young ladies, there was a brutal contrast between the comfort of their châteaux or sumptuous Paris apartments and the convent's conditions. The dormitories were cold as ice, the classrooms were disgustingly filthy, nauseating odors from the chicken coop permeated the classroom for the "little girls." Miss D***, "an old bogeyman in dirty petticoats,"[67] was their teacher, while Mother Alippe was in charge of their religious education. A young novice named Miss Hurst gave Aurore private English lessons every day in her cell.

The "little girls," between the ages of five and twelve, were divided into three categories, the "good girls," the "dummies," and the "devils." The leader of the "devils" was Mary Gillibrand, "an eleven-year-old Irish girl, much bigger and stronger than I was at the age of thirteen. She owed her nickname of *boy* to her booming voice, frank, impudent face, and independent, untamable character."[68] When they first met, Mary pummeled Aurore with questions: "The little miss is named Du pain? bread? Aurore's her name? rising sun? . . . what pretty names! and what a pretty face! Like a horse's head on a hen's back. Sunrise, I bow before you; I wish to be the sunflower greeting your first rays. . . . The whole class burst out laughing. The dummies especially were laughing hard enough to unhinge their jaws. The good girls were delighted to see two devils going after each other because they were afraid of them."[69]

This astonishingly rude introduction nevertheless signaled the beginning of a great friendship. Aurore immediately joined the "devils." Under the guidance of the dauntless Mary, they made some wild forays in the great architectural hodgepodge of the convent, a "labyrinth of roofs, overhangs, gables, attics, everything covered with mossy tiles and ramshackle chimneys."[70] Aurore remembered scary stories while Mary and her compatriots had come with their heads chock-full of terrifying Scottish and Irish legends. They would share tales about a woman being held captive in some inaccessible place and then go looking for her; they dreamed of garret rooms with hidden treasure and organized nocturnal forays to go find it. Sometimes the sorties came to an abrupt or unfortunate end, with punishments for the ringleaders, Dupin and Gillibrand, and a severe scolding for the others, but usually they ended in uncontrollable fits of giggles.

The Bibliothèque historique de la ville de Paris has an English spelling manual, the *Mavor Spelling Book*, that was Aurore Dupin's in 1818, the year she entered the convent. It is covered in pen annotations such as "*Isabella Clifford is charming*," "Mlle Anne de Wismes est une petite mimie" ["Miss Anne de Wismes is a little darling"], "À bas les Anglais" ["Down with the English"], or "Je suis enchantée de ne plus être dans la petite classe" ["I am delighted not to be in the little girls class any longer"]. On the flip side of the last page the pupil wrote: "This respectable and interesting book belongs to the worthy Dupin, otherwise known as the illustrious marquis of Sainte-Lucy, the five-star general of the convent's French army, a great warrior, a clever captain and intrepid soldier, crowned with oak and laurel in battle, defender of the oriflamme."[71]

This rhetoric of defense and conquest belongs to the world of men. How can one not succumb to it as soon as the imagination starts dreaming of glory, warfare, and military decorations? The daughter of a soldier, Aurore was already cross-dressing and changing her name—as a joke. Lots of other little girls have done the same thing since.

During her first months at the English convent, Aurore was bouncing back and forth between the exuberant pranks of a little gang of schoolgirls and utter dejection at the thought of her family. Her grandmother gave her news of Nohant on a regular basis and poured out all kinds of advice (we only have Marie-Aurore Dupin's letters). She would repeat: "For so long as I live, I'll celebrate your birthday as long as you console me for losing the man to whom you owe your life; and I hope to receive that consolation in the form of your efforts to develop your talents, your good behavior, and your gratitude toward your good mama to whom you are very dear."[72] These were the terms of the pact of consolation sealed at the time of Maurice's death, a pact the little girl was never allowed to forget.

After a few months in class with the "little girls," Aurore, even though she was rather unruly, was invited to move up with the "big girls." Her time as a "devil," when she often wore a *nightcap* as a sign of punishment,[73] was followed by a stretch of great serenity and the discovery of another world, that of devotion and humility, grace and mysticism.

Up until then Aurore had known little about religion. Like Deschartres, who claimed to be a materialist in the name of science, her grandmother had always sided with the "philosophers," considering Catholicism a fusty set of beliefs and practices. Even so, she was careful to respect decorum during the early years of the Restoration when religion was making an ostensible comeback and Jesuit schools were reopening, and she thought she ought to have her granddaughter prepared for communion. After a week of instruction by Nohant's ignoramus parish priest, Aurore knew her catechism by heart. On the appointed day she took communion under the watchful eye of her grandmother who was setting foot in the church of Nohant for the first time since her son's wedding: "All this was a puzzle to me; I was waiting for her [the grandmother] to really tell me about what she had made me do and the feeling she had shown. There was nothing of the sort. I was made to take communion again a week later, and then nobody ever said another word to me about religion, as if nothing had ever happened."[74] Aurore was thirteen. Religion, understood this way, was a mere formality, and communion, just a matter of etiquette.

While this first encounter with Catholicism left her with no lasting impression, Aurore would create for herself "an inner world to [her] liking, a fantastic and poetic world . . . , religious and philosophical,"[75] animated by a character of many shapes and forms that she named Corambé. To this "sort of god of [her] invention"[76] Aurore would confide her sorrows and hopes, imagining for hours and hours "scores of novels that would sink back into nothingness without ever being finished,"[77] all of them with Corambé as their hero. A condensation of many things that Aurore had found in books, Corambé owed something to Jesus, but also to the beauty of the Angel Gabriel, the grace of Orpheus, the determination of Ulysses, the courage of the "warrior Clorinda"[78] (the heroine of Tasso's *Jerusalem Delivered*), as well as to a few attributes of Sand's mother. A kind of companion, both male and female, Corambé figures in all the fables Aurore would tirelessly invent, rethinking and refining them in her moments of loneliness, boredom, and melancholy.

Corambé would amount to a mere anecdote if it didn't occupy such a huge place in *Story of My Life*. Sand is one of the rare autobiographers to recognize the workings of imagination in early adolescence. In her opinion, Corambé, "and with this creature, the thousands of others that soothed me every day with their pleasant daydreams,"[79] gave birth to her talent for writing novels, encouraging her to invent an imaginary universe, to play around with the characters there and invent adventures, to experiment with all the various narrative possibilities. Corambé was not just a central feature in the future writer's relationship with literary creation. Corambé may also, and perhaps most importantly, have functioned as a defense mechanism thanks to which the little girl, torn between her mother and her grandmother, could express her irrepressible need for love to a perfectly imaginary being. From what she says, Corambé "endlessly consoled and made things right,"[80] regulating unbearably strong inner tensions and slowly fostering greater resiliency in Corambé's creator.

When *Indiana* was published, Corambé and his imaginary universe grew dim and then disappeared: "[These dear visions] cruelly absconded to the bottom of my inkwell," Sand declared; "this half-hallucinatory phenomenon . . . totally vanished and all at once."[81] Thanks to her writing and publishing, the powerful shadow play of her youth was no longer needed. "George Sand" clearly went on to replace Corambé.

At the convent Aurore first engaged in all kinds of eccentricities, then saw how inane they were. She needed something else, "an ardent passion"[82] that would give her life meaning, a powerful feeling that would anchor itself to an object. Now it was God that she entreated when she found herself up against emotions too painful to bear and women too difficult to please: "I was fifteen. All my needs were in my heart, and my heart was bored. . . . I had no feeling of personality. . . . I needed to love beyond myself, and I knew of nothing on earth that I could love with all my might."[83]

The religious sentiment that was going to grip the adolescent and inspire her fervent devotion had a visual prompt. At the back of the chancel in the convent chapel there was a painting by Titian representing Jesus in the Garden of Gethsemane.[84] There was another interesting painting of the convent's patron saint, "Saint Augustine, under the fig tree, with the miraculous ray of light showing the famous words *Tolle, legge* ['Take, read'], these mysterious words . . . that made him decide to open the holy Gospel."[85] The story of a voice leading to conversion as well as the tale of Saint Paul hearing God's famous apostrophe, *Cur me persequeris?* ["Why are you persecuting me?"], on the road to Damascus are moving images, tales of sudden illumination that radically change one's destiny. Everything was in place so that Aurore too could be touched by grace. One evening, as she was about to leave the chapel, she suddenly felt overcome by a "feeling of terror and rapture."[86] That was it: "I felt . . . that I loved God, that my mind embraced and totally accepted this ideal of justice, love, and holiness."[87]

Aurore was essentially overcome by religious "feeling." This period had taken back up with a sense of religion more inspired by Rousseau's Savoyard vicar than by the Catholic clergy that since the Concordat, and even more after the return of the Bourbon kings, had regained all its prerogatives. Even so, once the Catholic Church had again taken charge of girls' education, the practice of religion started up afresh, which did a lot to instill the girls with the "natural virtues" their parents wished them to have. The century that had prided itself on attacking Catholicism was now far in the past, with Diderot's forthright materialism and Voltaire's battles against the power of the clergy and more general denunciation of all religion as imposture. The same could be said of the iconoclastic philosophy of the French Revolution. Most Romantic authors would invoke God and, like Rousseau, see the irrefutable sign of God's presence in nature, love, and all forms of beauty: "Have no doubt," the hero of *The Confession of a Child of the Century* [*La confession d'un enfant du siècle*] declared to his beloved, "Providence has led me to you. . . . God has sent you as an angel of light to rescue me from the abyss. You have been entrusted with this saintly mission."[88]

After her conversion Aurore left the "devils" for the coterie of devout girls. She made a complete confession to the convent chaplain, Abbot de Prémord, and took communion the following day. Then began a period of ardent mysticism: "I was literally burning like Saint Theresa; I stopped eating and sleeping, I walked around totally unaware of the movements of my body. . . . In a word, I was in ecstasy, my body had no feeling, it no longer existed. My thoughts took strange, impossible turns. Was I even thinking? No, mystics don't think. They live in an endless dream, they contemplate, they aspire, they burn, they are consumed, and they wouldn't know how to describe this mode of existence, which is quite special and can't be compared to anything else."[89] Aurore became friends with one of the convent's young nuns, Sister Helen, and soon became convinced that she had to take religious orders. She folded altar linens, rehearsed chorales and motets in the organ loft, spent lots of time in the novices' room, even going so far as to choose her spot in the little cemetery beside the convent chapel.

This extravagant behavior did not escape the attention of her confessor, an enlightened Jesuit. He disapproved of all kinds of religious excesses and told Aurore to live in the present without worrying too much just then about her future vocation. She didn't need much coaxing. Soon she was composing charades, theater sketches, and little morality plays that were performed by a few students under her direction. On the Mother Superior's name day she even put on a sugar-coated and much abbreviated version of Molière's *The Imaginary Invalid* [*Le malade imaginaire*]: "Total success, people couldn't have been more enthusiastic!"[90] From then on, she would never stop writing plays. The nuns were delighted to have a new kind of devout girl, "cooperative and fun."[91] The "devils" agreed with the "good girls" that this God-fearing girl was fine company. Mysticism was now far away!

Yet Aurore was still thinking about taking religious vows. Her grandmother who often visited Aurore in the convent parlor on her visits to Paris wound up fearing she might actually do it. As

Aurore's guardian, she decided to take her out of the convent of English Sisters and back to Nohant: "This news hit me like a bolt of lightning, in the midst of the most perfect happiness I had ever known in my life. The convent had become my paradise on earth. There I was neither a pupil nor a nun, but something in between, with absolute liberty within walls that I cherished, that I was sorry to leave, even for a day. . . . I was friends with everybody, the councilor and leader for all the fun, the little ones' idol." She had no choice but to obey. Brokenhearted, Aurore left the convent on 12 April 1820. She was just fifteen.

These two years at the convent in rue des Fossés-Saint-Victor were pivotal. No doubt she hadn't learned much with the English Augustinian Sisters, and she would complain bitterly about this later on, but her life was calmer, merrier, more like that of girls of her age and class than her life at Nohant in the wake of her father's death. Freed from the torment caused by the bad blood between an authoritarian grandmother and a loving, but terribly impulsive mother, freed as well from Deschartres's capricious schooling, she had gained autonomy and self-confidence. She had been able to *choose*—to be a "devil" or a good girl, to become friends with this or that student, to think up some practical joke or plunge into pious reflections. From what she says in *Story of My Life*, it seems that her temperament was then more or less set for life: on the one hand, resolutely open, sociable, generous to a point of self-abnegation; on the other, intrinsically anxious, always keen to transcend reality in some way or other. Her future conduct would remain deeply marked by these traits.

Back in Nohant, life took shape as it could. Aurore's grandmother was less and less well. Deschartres was still there, but he was often busy outside. A certain Monsieur Lacoux served as Aurore's English tutor and briefly gave her harp and guitar lessons. Now an army officer, Hippolyte Chatiron returned to Nohant on leave from time to time, as his father had done. Even so, the grandmother did not treat Maurice's two children equally: Aurore "did not owe" a bastard "respect,"[92] she reminded her granddaughter in a letter. "The child from the little house" gave the child from the château her first riding lessons: "Hang on to the mane if you wish, but don't go let go of the bridle and don't fall off," he recommended. "That's the whole thing: you fall off or you don't."[93] She didn't fall off and was soon riding with great pleasure.

She was delighted to get back to her room at Nohant and the garden, to hear once again "the plowman's timeless and solemn cantilena."[94] Yet this did not prevent keen anxiety and deep sadness, "a pathological hopelessness"[95] that made Aurore shed bitter tears. Why? She herself didn't understand and left the question unanswered at the time.

There remained her friendships from the convent. These generated lots of letters and a few visits. Pauline de Pontcarré and her mother spent several weeks at Nohant during the summer of 1820. On 15 August, Mme Dupin's name day, the two girls performed one of Carmontelle's little morality plays in which Aurore, dressed as a boy, took the role of Colin while Pauline played the amorous Colette. Everybody enjoyed it.

A few friends from the convent, Jane and Aimée Bazouin, Appolonie de Bruges, and Émilie de Wismes, were among Aurore's regular correspondents. They exchanged well-turned urbanities: "Who is this writing to me? What is this stamp? whose handwriting? in short, this person whom I don't know? . . . Come now, my dear, you know it's your friend from the convent, and knowing that you're back home with your family, as you were wishing for so long, I wanted to offer my regards and congratulations."[96] They talked about the people they had met at the convent, and sprinkled bits of English over their French: "Yes, my fine Wismes, I was delighted *at hearing* this happy news [her return home] and I once again congratulate you on the pleasure of having Miss Gabb [a lay teacher from the convent] as governess. I saw Louisa *there some time ago*."[97] They recounted the day's little events to each other and ended with the usual endearments: "I *kiss* you and your sister a thousand times. Another day I'll write you both a really long letter and, of course, the loveliest ever. Write to me. I love you dearly, my fine Émilie, and hug you once again."[98]

All this no doubt testifies to the pervasive influence of epistolary etiquette among upper-class young ladies, and all its conventions. Yet Aurore's letters to her friends soon began to show a remarkable talent for observation, a touch of originality when reporting comic scenes occasionally put in dialogue form, plus a desire to reflect about life and to make general statements about behavior. They are indisputably different from the "so lovely"[99] letters she received. Aurore was appropriating a form of writing that she would soon use with ease. She was breaking in a tone, a style, a personal way of *expressing* reality in the written word.

One rarely becomes a writer for having composed, even very well, scores of witty and original letters to friends and acquaintances. Still, before Sand tried her hand at novels, a great letter-writer was being born, and she would prove particularly voluble, faithful in friendship, generous with details about her life and feelings, not to mention her religious and political convictions. In manuscript form (or lost but attested) there are now some 19,600 letters written by George Sand.[100] The first was addressed to Sophie Dupin in 1812 when she was eight; the last was addressed to her nephew, Oscar Cazamajou, on 30 May 1876, a few days before she died.

DOLDRUMS AND DREAMS

In early 1821 Aurore's grandmother, feeling that her strength was waning and her health failing, wanted to find a husband for her granddaughter, now going on seventeen. She consulted with old friends and quickly scanned the various possibilities. Her cousin, René de Villeneuve who owned the château of Chenonceaux, suggested one of Napoleon's generals: "This fifty-year-old looks nearly as young as I do [Villeneuve was thirty-four]. He is intelligent, well educated, in short, everything necessary for a happy marriage; for there are lots of young men out there, but one can never be sure of their character, and their future is most uncertain; whereas this one has everything, status, money, and respect."[101] One by one, the candidates were all rejected, some by the grandmother, others by

Aurore, who felt terribly anxious about getting married. At the end of February Marie-Aurore Dupin had a stroke. Paralyzed on one side of her body, she was confined to bed while her granddaughter read to her at length. For the time being, any marriage plans were abandoned.

Managed one way or another by a disabled old lady and a very ignorant girl, Nohant fell all of a sudden into a strange state of torpor. Indeed, when Deschartres was reunited with his former pupil, he did not mince words. It only took a few conversations with Aurore for him to judge her "crassly ignorant."[102] Miffed, she decided to try to teach herself something and got into the habit of working by herself at night, "from ten until two or three in the morning."[103]

At the convent she had loved reading novels, but now it was especially serious works that got her attention. *The Imitation of Christ* [*L'imitation de Jésus-Christ*, generally attributed to Thomas à Kempis] became her bedside reading, and she discovered Chateaubriand's *The Genius of Christianity* [*Le génie du christianisme*], which she soon came to love "passionately,"[104] nor did she stop there. Taking great interest in matters of religion and theology, she decided to "read everything . . . , all the philosophers, all the nonbelievers, all the heretics, full of the sweet certainty that their errors would confirm and guarantee my own faith."[105] The few letters she exchanged with Abbot Prémord, who had once saved her from religious exaltation, show how keenly interested she was in all things religious and political. It would be impossible to understand some of her great future novels, such as *Consuelo* or *Mademoiselle La Quintinie*, without gauging Sand's youthful interest in religion and the history of Christianity, including its errors and faulty judgments. Sand would wind up choosing the Protestant faith for herself and her family, and already late in adolescence, she was tirelessly asking herself about the nature of religious feeling, the conditions for the collective practice of religion, its articles of faith, and the role of the clergy.

Soon her curiosity was aroused by the whole of Marie-Aurore Dupin's vast library. With her irrepressible desire for knowledge, she read everything she could get her hands on, theologians and philosophers, thinkers and the great writers of classic texts from France and elsewhere, in other words, the compendium of knowledge and taste in the second half of the eighteenth century. Aurore was using these books to try to understand what to do with the rest of her life, whether she should get married or preferred to take religious orders: "Onward! onward! . . . I unceremoniously tackled Mably, Locke, Condillac, Montesquieu, Bacon, Bossuet, Aristotle, Leibniz, Pascal, Montaigne. . . . Then came the poets and the moralists: La Bruyère, Pope, Milton, Dante, Virgil, Shakespeare, what have you. Everything without rhyme or reason, as I came upon them. . . . To my eyes this was all a question of life or death, namely, after understanding everything I could propose to understand, whether I would go into life in society or into death in the cloister."[106]

In the midst of all this reading followed by vigorous discussions with Deschartres, who was still hostile to religion, Aurore discovered Jean-Jacques Rousseau. She was dazzled: "Jean-Jacques's language and the form of his reasoning grabbed me like a superb piece of music lit up by a giant sun. He was like Mozart to me; I could understand everything."[107] Sand's points of view on politics, religion, and education would bear the lasting mark of *Julie, or the New Eloise* [*La nouvelle Héloïse*], of theories developed in *The Social Contract* [*Le contrat social*] or *Émile*. She would restate her immense admiration for Rousseau, plus a bit of criticism, in her preface to a new edition of his *Confessions* in 1841.[108]

Aurore Dupin did not content herself with spending the night reading and acquiring "principles"[109] that would become the basis of all her future thinking. On her mare Colette she rode around the countryside in men's clothing and sometimes made a game of passing herself off as a "monsieur," as she wrote in a letter to Émilie de Wismes.[110] Clearly, cross-dressing, the tone and manners that went along with it, held a powerful charm for her. "How simple it seemed to me," she would recall, "not to live like most girls."[111] What a scandal in and around La Châtre! The "horseman's" clothes, her hunting, her love of learning, her chumminess with young men her age, made tongues wag, and Deschartres told her to be more careful. "There she is, our young lady, galloping about on her huge horse; she's got to be crazy to do things like that,"[112] people would exclaim in the Berry countryside.

To her mother, who worried at least as much about her "running around"[113] as her desire for learning, she wrote: "I am extremely surprised that you, my mother, take a dim view of my educating myself. No doubt you think a woman has more useful things to do, things more akin to housework, which is a woman's duty. Why must a woman be ignorant? Can't she be educated without bragging about it or acting like a bluestocking?"[114] This is the first time such a question crops up in her letters. It shows the mentality of the time—which still made fun of educated women, with people accusing them of preferring pedantry to the *duties* of their sex—as well as the strength of character required to break free of it and decide to learn something *even so*.

Yet one sore point would trouble her for quite a while yet: "My melancholy became . . . dejection, and my dejection, pain. That's just one step away from disgust with life and desire for death. My home life was so dreary, so agonizing, my body so irritated by a constant battle against depression, my brain so weary of solemn thoughts too advanced for my youth and books too engrossing for my age, that I found myself facing a very serious spiritual affliction: the temptation of suicide."[115] Aurore went on in greater detail: "Water especially held a mysterious charm for me. I wouldn't walk anywhere but along the river, . . . following it like an automaton to some deep spot. Then, stopped on the bank and seemingly magnetized in place, I would feel a burst of fever in my head and tell myself: 'How easy it would be! One more step, and that's it! . . .' I would start asking myself: Yes or no? often enough and long enough to run the risk of the 'yes' hurling me down into that limpid, magnetizing water."[116] One day she thought she heard the "fatal yes,"[117] and into the deep water she went with her mare. She was saved by her mare Colette's survival instinct and Deschartres's fast work. He read her the riot act while huge tears rolled down her face. She swore not to do it again. They started talking again, now about free will and the strange fits of mind that can sometimes jeopardize reason.

On 26 December 1821 Mme Dupin de Francueil died at Nohant, bequeathing her entire estate to her granddaughter: the house at Nohant, the three farms and more than two hundred hectares of farmland, a townhouse in Paris (the so-called hôtel de Narbonne), and a few apartments. René de Villeneuve had been named Aurore's guardian and the manager of her property up until the time she was married. Sophie Dupin arrived in Nohant a few days later. She wrongly suspected Deschartres of embezzlement, making loud and clear how pleased she was to see her mother-in-law six feet under. Soon she took her daughter back to Paris where she moved into the apartment in rue Neuve-des-Mathurins.

It soon became clear that it would not be easy for them to live together. Sophie Dupin had no patience for the things her daughter, until quite recently a student at one of the best convents in Paris, was interested in and wanted to talk about, nor did she appreciate Aurore's feelings for her grandmother. This brief time with her mother let Aurore take full measure of everything that would henceforth separate her from the woman whose presence and love she had once so fervently desired.

While visiting friends of her grandmother at the château of Plessis-Picard, near Melun in April 1822, Aurore met a "slim, rather elegant young man with a jolly face and military bearing."[118] Twenty-seven years old, Casimir Dudevant was the son of a maid and a retired colonel, a baron of the Empire. His father recognized him at birth, and Colonel Dudevant's wife raised the baby as her own, in a sort of rosy version of Hippolyte Chatiron's story. When he met Aurore, Casimir was a second lieutenant and had just finished his law degree. He lived with his parents in the department of Lot-et-Garonne in the château of Guillery, "a little house with five windows . . . , furnished like all the houses in southern France, very modestly."[119]

Aurore saw him several more times, in Paris and at the house of the Roëttiers du Plessis family where she spent the summer. Casimir Dudevant did not keep his plans hidden long. Like the

to work to deliver a great history lesson about France on the eve of the Revolution, a political reading of the role of social class, money, and property, fresh insights about marriage, family, and women. The descriptions of the countryside around the village of Sainte-Sévère, the rural world of the Old Regime, the relationships between dishonest little country squires and the peasants that depended on them, are wonderfully precise, and the discussions among the characters sum up the great intellectual debates in the years before the Revolution. Yet Sand "idealized" two aspects of the novel: first, by creating a very knowledgeable heroine who becomes the teacher of the man she is going to marry—up until then novels had tended to prefer things the other way around—and second, by ending her novel with the portrayal of life in community. Once the revolutionary storm was over, Edmée and Bernard share their life, their château, and their property with a few friends from every class of society, the heroine ever "faithful to her theories of absolute equality."[73]

This defense of marriage, and celebration of the ideals of equality and community, were something new. They directly relate to convictions that Sand's subsequent novels were going to set forth more and more clearly. Sand would no longer be accused of writing to express her "hatred of marriage,"[74] nor would she go on publishing novels about unhappy marriages and adultery for the sake of love, as Balzac did time and time again. These times were over. Now Sand was indisputably considered a novelist and definitively freed from the tutelage of a contemptible husband, and after a few great intellectual encounters, plus a few momentous affairs, her fiction took on political, ethical, and religious convictions, and she was henceforth committed to more didactic ends.

These intellectual debates left an eloquent mark on her novels, and her long, detailed letters to numerous correspondents produced a lively echo chamber of the same. In the midst of all this, Sand found the time to travel, to love, to look after her children as well as Nohant, to entertain friends, and to indulge her love of reading, walking, and music.

In August 1836 she asked her maid to pack her bags:

My old Tortoise, pack me up—my men's shirts, I've only got two.—buy me two colored ones . . .
—my velvet riding coat.
—all my trousers
—40 francs of corn-paper cigarettes
—two chemical lighters . . .
—a pair of very loose-fitting slippers that I can wear traveling with swollen feet . . .
—my foulard dress and the sleeves of my flowered gray dress. . . . Plus, my lacework and my veil.
—two toothbrushes, soft rather than hard . . .
—2 cakes of honey soap.[75]

Along with Maurice, now thirteen, and Solange, soon to turn eight, Sand went to Chamonix to join Franz Liszt and Marie d'Agoult, whom she had met a few months earlier. For this occasion, Liszt and his companion were nicknamed the Longfellows, Sand and her children the Piffoëls. Marie d'Agoult recalled in her *Memoirs* [*Mémoires*]:

Madame Sand was very short and seemed even shorter in the men's clothes she wore with ease and not without a certain youthful, manly grace. Neither the development of her bust nor the curves of her hips betrayed her sex. The black velvet riding coat tight around her waist, the heeled boots on her little feet with their high arches, the necktie around her full, round neck . . . let her move freely. With all that, her forthright demeanor gave the idea of quiet strength. . . . There was something strange about the beauty of her dark eyes, her hair as well. She seemed to see without looking and . . . her gaze was impenetrable; an unsettling calm, something cold like our ideas of the sphinxes of Antiquity.[76]

Sand wrote this trip up twice: first, as an open letter that appeared in the *Revue des Deux Mondes* like the previous ones; it is the tenth of Sand's *Traveler's Letters* and contains some charming observations about Maurice and Solange in the mountains.[77] She composed another version as a diary entitled *Daily Chats with*

*the Very Learned and Very Clever Doctor Piffoël Professor of Botany
and Psychology* [*Entretiens journaliers avec le très docte et très habile
docteur Piffoël professeur de botanique et de psychologie*], never published during her lifetime.[78] These texts mirror each other, each
one donning the clothes of the "traveler" to hail Liszt's genius
("How soothing when Franz plays the piano. All my troubles turn
to poetry, all my instincts are elated."[79]) and to jeer at Lélia ("Never
take a strong, selfless, courageous, wide-eyed soul as your ideal
woman. The public will hiss and boo, greeting you with the odious
name of Lélia, the feckless one!"[80]). It is not easy to be double: a
strong woman and a man of letters.

During the following winter and spring, Franz Liszt and Marie
d'Agoult made two lengthy stays at Nohant. An attentive observer of
these distinguished guests, Maurice sketched his mother in profile,
with a fascinated eye and a cigarette in her mouth, standing behind
Liszt at the piano, with his angular body and long, fluttering fingers;
the sketch was captioned: "Mama amazed to be hearing Liszt."[81]
Franz Liszt dedicated the third of his *Letters of a Bachelor in Music*
[*Lettres d'un bachelier ès musique*] to his stay at Nohant. He wrote:

> I went to seek refuge in the farthest reaches of Berry, that prosaic
> province so divinely turned to poetry by George Sand. There,
> under the roof of our illustrious friend, for three months long I
> lived a rich life full of feeling. . . . These were our pursuits and
> pleasures: reading some ingenuous philosopher, profound poet
> . . . , or letter from a faraway friend; long walks on the secret
> banks of the Indre; . . . the joyful shrieks of the children who
> had just discovered a lovely hawk moth with diaphanous wings
> or some poor warbler . . . fallen from its nest down in the grass.
> And that's all? Yes, in truth, that's all. . . . The soul's joys are not
> to be measured by how wide they are, but how deep.[82]

Sand felt great admiration and real friendship for Lizst, and he
shared these sentiments. In 1836 the composer dedicated *Rondo
fantastique*[83] "to Monsieur George Sand," which she "translated"
as a short story entitled *The Smuggler* [*Le contrebandier*]. Later on,

when evoking the beginning of his relationship with Chopin in the 1852 biography devoted to him, Franz Liszt described Sand-Lélia in these terms:

> Lélia with your brown hair and olive skin! you wandered through solitary places, somber like Lara, torn like Manfred [two of Byron's heroes], rebellious like Cain, but fiercer and more pitiless, more inconsolable than they were, for there has not been a man's heart feminine enough to love you as they have been loved, to pay your virile charms the homage of trusting and blind submission, of wordless and ardent devotion, to let your Amazon strength protect his expressions of submission! Woman-hero, you have been valiant and eager for combat like these war-riors. . . . Like them, you had to armor . . . this female breast, which, charming as life itself, discreet as the tomb, is adored by man when his heart is its sole and impenetrable shield.[84]

As for "Arabella," Sand appreciated the refined aristocrat and accomplished musician that she was. In particularly glowing terms she dedicated *Simon* to her friend and marveled at what first struck her as "incommensurable superiority."[85] Marie d'Agoult, mean-while, did not hide her admiration for the independent woman, talented artist, and generous friend who entertained them so simply at Nohant. Yet the little brunette and the tall blonde were radically different. Endowed with more native talent, Sand soon grew impatient with Marie d'Agoult's inflexible thinking as well as her posing as a woman of society. Marie d'Agoult began to feel jealous of the influence Sand's strong personality exercised over the people around her, including Liszt.

Their friendship, quite intense at the beginning—so much so that people thought for a moment that George was in love with Marie—would deteriorate bit by bit and come to an end after various calumnies reached Sand's ears. "Your understanding of friendship is different from mine," she wrote to Marie d'Agoult in November 1839, ". . . you just won't give up being a beautiful and witty woman who slaughters and smashes all the others."[86] The rivalry between the two women would inspire Balzac to write his novel *Béatrix*, and Sand modeled the Viscountess de Chailly in her novel *Horace* on Marie d'Agoult. Sand's influence, as Marie d'Agoult would herself acknowledge, helped her decide on the literary career of which she had been dreaming,[87] and she too chose a masculine pen name. Marie d'Agoult had real talent, even if she seemed more comfortable writing essays rather than novels. Published under the name "Daniel Stern" in 1847, her *Essay on Liberty* [*Essai sur la liberté*] is original in a number of ways.

After her breakup with Michel de Bourges who became "absorbed by a new passion"[88] in the spring of 1838, Sand was keen to find another lover. The actor Pierre-François Touzé, known as Bocage, the writer Charles Didier, then the vaudevillist Félicien Mallefille, hired as Sand's secretary and Maurice's tutor, shared her affection one after the other. This bothered Franz Liszt and Marie d'Agoult during their stays at Nohant, and sometimes her best friends failed to understand. It is clear that Sand gladly yielded to the pleasure of being seduced, possessed, and loved. She also greatly enjoyed seducing, becoming one with whoever pleased her and returning the feeling: "Love bubbles in me like the sap of life in the universe," she wrote to Michel de Bourges. "The beloved's breast is the only pillow able to give repose to both body and soul."[89] Love and everything that went along with it corresponded to a need that nothing or nobody would ever be able to fulfill. Never failing to evoke love as a vital principle, Sand was constantly giddy with desire to feel restored through fusion with another. An impossible dream, but no less stubbornly pursued.

Still, with regard to love and everything else humans do, one must think and ask questions. With rare frankness Sand would discuss all these things with her correspondents, reminding them in no uncertain terms of the contradictions in which women of her time found themselves. Neither did she ever let them forget the weight of opinion always ready to blame them:

Opinion, on the one hand, doesn't tolerate ugly, cold, or cowardly women; on the other, it is the voice of reviling, mocking, and insulting men who no longer want devout women, who don't yet want enlightened women, and still want faithful women. . . . So women now are not enlightened, devout, or chaste; the moral revolution that was supposed to remake them according to the desires of the new generation of men went haywire. They didn't want to raise women in their own eyes; they didn't want to give women a noble role and put them on an equal footing that would make them capable of manly virtues. Chastity would have been glorious for free women. For enslaved women, it is mutilating tyranny, a yoke they're trying hard to shake off. I can't blame them.[90]

Here her views dovetail with those of Pierre Leroux, who had become the advocate of a standpoint whose "very essence was equality."[91] As for Sand's conduct with regard to her relationships, she would still be implacably judged. "Latrine,"[92] jabbed Baudelaire, one of the first; "a monster whore,"[93] Alexandre Dumas fils confided (is this really so?) to the Goncourt brothers, who would smugly take note in their *Journal*.

In early March 1838, Sand entertained Balzac at Nohant, and he eagerly reported the visit to Mme Hanska: "I found the comrade Georges [*sic*] Sand in her dressing gown smoking a cigar after supper near the fire. . . . She was wearing pretty yellow slippers with a fringe, elegant little stockings, and red trousers. . . . For three days we chatted from five in the evening after supper until five in the morning. . . . She was . . . even more unhappy with Musset [than with Sandeau]. Her men are few and far between, that's the story. All the more so because she is not at all lovable. . . . She's a boy, an artist, she is great, generous, dedicated, *chaste*, she has the fine traits of a man, *ergo* she is no woman."[94] Balzac reported to Mme Hanska that Sand seemed to have no real vision, no talent for planning her novels, nor any ability to portray truth or feeling. Yet he recognized that "without knowing the French language, she has *style*."[95]

Together Sand and Balzac talked about marriage. Balzac was convinced that the husband had to be superior to the wife, which was Rousseau's position in *Émile*. On the pretext that he understood women better than anybody (many other novelists after

Balzac would boast of the same talent), Balzac represented women as devoted to the point of sacrifice, desperate when they understood that they had been betrayed and abandoned, deeply religious as well. "Feeling, loving, and suffering,"[96] that is their destiny, he reminded his readers in *Eugénie Grandet*. Sand totally disagreed. The novels that she wrote at this time, *The Last Aldini* [*La dernière Aldini*] and *The Master Mosaic Makers* [*Les maîtres mosaïstes*], are no doubt marked by memories of Italy. Still, no more than in *Mauprat*, there was never any question of portraying heroines who did not consider themselves equal to the men they loved.

Despite Balzac's gossip with Mme Hanska about Sand, in particular, about the many lovers he chalked up to her, this fundamental difference did not interfere with their special bond. Sand occupies a particular place in the novels of *The Human Comedy*. In *The County Muse* [*La muse du département*] he invented the term "Sandism" to evoke a new way of life and behavior; in *Béatrix*, he modeled Camille Maupin on Sand; he would leave unfinished a novel entitled *The Woman Author* [*La femme auteur*]. He was obviously fascinated by Sand's talent, originality, and prodigious capacity for work, by the exception she was in all respects.

In 1842 Balzac dedicated his *Letters from Two Young Brides* [*Lettres de deux jeunes mariées*] to Sand. After reading it, she immediately wrote to him: "The book is one of the most beautiful things you've ever written. I don't arrive at your conclusions, and I think instead that you prove quite the opposite of what you intend to demonstrate. All great minds feel the pros and cons of everything so intensely, so ingenuously. . . . I dream of writing a long article about you . . . perhaps contradicting you more in a thousand things than you've ever been before and exalting you higher than anybody else ever has. No one has ever understood you, I think, and I think I understand you well."[97] Maybe this declaration was the reason why Balzac would a few months later ask Sand to write the preface to *The Human Comedy* when this work was finally coming all together. What fine homage to his "comrade" Sand! This project fell by the wayside, and Balzac would wind up writing the twenty-six pages of his famous preface by himself.[98]

In 1840 the German artist Josef Danhauser executed a huge oil painting on wood entitled *Morning with Liszt* [*La matinée chez Liszt*], now at the Nationalgalerie in Berlin. Facing a bust of Beethoven, Liszt is playing the piano, and Marie d'Agoult, with her back turned, is sitting on a cushion at his feet. Wearing a long skirt and a riding coat, Sand is stretched out in an armchair, daydreaming; she is holding a cigarette in her left hand and giving her right hand to Alexandre Dumas, sitting beside her. Victor Hugo, apparently lost in thought, is standing behind them with a book in his hands, while Rossini has a hand on Paganini's shoulder. A perfectly improbable scene, but it has the merit of bringing together a few of the great names in European music and literature of the time and demonstrating the tremendous fame that George Sand had come to enjoy. Her works were then being translated into English, German, Dutch, Spanish, Italian, and Russian.

MUSIC

Sand wrote to Franz Liszt that her passion for music would throw her "into otherworldly states of ecstasy and rapture."[99] She reminded Marie d'Agoult that she liked to lie under the piano while Liszt was playing: "I'm made of very strong fiber, and I never find instruments powerful enough. Besides, [Liszt] is the only artist in the world who can give soul and life to the piano."[100] Already as a child she used to crawl beneath the spinet, charmed as she was by her grandmother singing and playing some old tune.[101] As she wrote, "Ah! how I'd sometimes love to be fifteen and have a smart music teacher and my whole life for me alone! I'd give myself totally to music, and it's in that language, the most perfect of all, that I'd express my feelings and emotions."[102]

Most Romantic authors were no doubt music lovers. Stendhal put Mozart, Cimarosa, and Rossini above all else and spent his evenings at the opera in Paris, Milan, and Rome. Alfred de Vigny entertained Liszt and Chopin at home and introduced them to each other. Another great music lover, Théophile Gautier wrote the arts column for several papers and reviewed Chopin's rare public concerts. Honoré de Balzac was not to be outdone; it suffices to recall the first pages of *La Duchesse de Langeais*, dedicated to Franz Liszt, and one will hear, admirably described, the *effect* of an organ piece. Music was all the rage, which was both good and bad: soporific musical soirées, idle discussions among "music lovers," lessons in piano and sensibility at home (for young ladies), nothing escaped the acerbic wit of Honoré Daumier, who published in *Le Charivari* the series entitled *Soirées parisiennes, Croquis musicaux*, and *Les musiciens de Paris*.

With her taste for music and interest in all its forms, Sand was one of the most accomplished musicians among authors. With her natural sensuality she found endlessly renewed emotions in voice, chant, and melody. In the country she loved bird songs, savoring that of the nightingale, which "strikes the heart with an electric shock,"[103] but still preferring the song of the blackbird, which "comes closer to our musical forms . . . , having phrases of a rustic ingenuity that one could almost write down and sing."[104] In *Teverino*, published in 1847, she created the charming character of the "bird-girl" who could attract hundreds of birds. "The bird-man," she wrote, "is the artist."[105]

In Paris Sand attended premieres of the operas of Berlioz and Meyerbeer—she dedicated the eleventh of her *Traveler's Letters* to the author of *Robert the Devil* [*Robert le diable*]. Later on she would attend Gounod's premieres and dream of writing an opera sketch for him. She was enchanted by the piano. At that time there was a lot of enthusiasm for this instrument, whose sonority had been markedly improved by the technical innovations of the manufacturers Sébastien Érard[106] and Camille Pleyel. Two virtuosi, the Hungarian Franz Liszt and the Pole Frederick Chopin, who could occasionally be heard playing together and who also played their own compositions, were applauded all over Europe.

Born in 1810 in a village a few kilometers outside of Warsaw, Chopin had a Polish mother and a French father who worked as a tutor for a prominent family. Very early on he showed exceptional talent. In 1829 he finished his studies at the Conservatory and gave a concert in Vienna that the critics hailed with enthusiasm. He went to Paris in 1831, the same year the German poet Heinrich Heine moved there. The frail, blue-eyed composer with delicate features, polished manners, and the elegance of a dandy never lost his pronounced Polish accent. He was already famous when Sand made his acquaintance. People vied for his lessons, crowded in to hear his latest compositions and to relish his tremendous skill as a performer.

Aside from a few public appearances, Chopin did not give concerts. In the presence of a chosen circle he preferred to play pieces by his favorite composers (Bach, Beethoven, Schubert) and occasionally a few of his own (or of Liszt). On 8 May 1838 Astolphe de Custine invited some famous men, politicians and artists, to hear a recital by Chopin at his house. Sand was among these guests.

Chopin and Sand had already met, but Chopin at first glance felt wary of this woman six years his senior and enjoying a solid reputation of freedom of every sort. Yet they took a liking to each other, said as much, and soon became lovers. "We surrendered to the wind, and it swept us both away to another realm for a few instants,"[107] Sand confessed to Albert Grzymala in a letter from the end of May 1838. Grzymala, the erstwhile aide-de-camp of Prince Poniatowski, who was exiled to France after the Polish revolution, was close to Chopin, and he would be the couple's confidant throughout their affair. Thanks to him, Sand was introduced to the circle of Polish refugees in Paris, among which there were some great aristocrats and intellectuals, such as the poet Adam Mickiewicz, "a genius equal to Byron,"[108] who held the chair of Slavic literature at the Collège de France.

When Sand met Chopin, she was still involved with Félicien Mallefille, and Chopin was emotionally attached to Maria Wodzinska and dreaming of getting engaged. This made Sand think twice about having a relationship with Chopin, as she explained to Grzymala: "Do I love as an artist, a woman, a sister, a nun, a poet, what on earth do I know? Some of my [feelings of love] have come to life and died the same day, without the person who inspired them ever knowing a thing about it. Some have been my martyrdom and driven me to despair, almost madness. Some have kept me cloistered for years in excessive spiritualism. They've all been perfectly sincere."[109] Something else worried her. Did Chopin prefer the communion of souls to communion between bodies? "In all sincerity, is there such a thing as . . . purely intellectual love? Is there ever love without a single kiss or a loving kiss without sensual delight?"[110] she wondered.

In any case, from June on, Sand and Chopin were inseparable. Sand was quite smitten and did not hide this from her correspondents. Truly in love, Chopin found in Sand generous feelings and also an exceptional sensitivity to music. "The poet and the musician"[111] were both famous, but Sand was the better known of the two. She frequented the artistic elite of Paris, and between the capital and her estate at Nohant she lived comfortably, mainly because of what she earned from her novels.

Their travel plans firmed up by the end of the summer of 1838. Chopin was then showing lung problems that already suggested tuberculosis, and Félicien Mallefille was threatening his former mistress. Spanish friends had recommended they stay on one of the Balearic islands off Barcelona, and on 18 October Sand went south with her two children. The travelers were in Avignon on 25 October, next they visited the fountain of Vaucluse and the arena at Nîmes. On the 29th they were in Perpignan, where Chopin joined them—the couple did not pass unnoticed and received a spontaneous ovation.[112] On 1 November they all embarked at Port-Vendres for Barcelona: "I'm so happy! [Chopin] is here, and healthy. . . . He looks fine, we're leaving in a few hours. The sky looks like Italy."[113] Chopin, Sand, Maurice, and Solange arrived at Palma on 8 November, first staying in a big house, So'n Vent, of which Maurice left a drawing. Then on 15 December they moved to an abandoned Carthusian monastery high in the mountains a few kilometers from the village of Valldemosa. They intended to stay there until the following spring. Sand wrote in an initial burst of enthusiasm: "The great charterhouse of Valldemosa . . . is poetry, solitude, the most artistic place ever, nothing more *chic* under the heavens, and what heavens! what a spot! we're just delighted. . . . It's the promised land, and we're overjoyed to have found ourselves a really fine place to stay. . . . Yesterday Chopin walked seven and a half miles with Maurice and us [Sand and Solange], over sharp stones. Both of them only feel better for it today. Solange and I are growing fat enough to inspire fear but not pity."[114]

Yet this second stay abroad had quite a few surprises in store for them. While Venice had for centuries been a vacation place for people of all nationalities, Majorca was a closed-minded little island where life was austere, religion powerful, and "tourism" nonexistent. "Just imagine," Sand wrote to Balzac, "a ferocious population, loyal as Carthaginians, fanatic as Spaniards."[115] Sand was expecting an endless summer; she found cool, often quite rainy weather, not very good for someone with tuberculosis. She dreamed of a land of liberty, open to the arts and welcoming to artists; she found herself in a very humble and perfectly traditional peasant setting. Moreover, the political situation of Spain was still chaotic, mainly because of French foreign policy since the Napoleonic Empire, and the peasants of Majorca preferred the conservatives, meaning the Carlists, who supported the brother of Ferdinand VII, to the liberals, who preferred Maria-Cristina de Bourbon.

The people of the island found these rich and famous strangers more and more staggering: the couple was not married, the family did not attend Sunday Mass, the musician was maybe suffering from a contagious disease and had a grand piano delivered from Paris. These people first excited their curiosity, then their hostility. There was incomprehension on both sides, then one incident after the other. *A Winter in Majorca* [*Un hiver à Majorque*] came out in 1842 and gives an account of their time there. Except for a few short passages, the work does not do justice to the special nature of Majorcan culture and comes down hard on the inhabitants. According to Sand, they were savages still back in the "age of the pig."[116] The work would not be well received in Spain—for good reason.[117]

Despite rather rudimentary living conditions and a steady cough, Chopin managed to finish in Majorca the twenty-four preludes, opus 28, dedicated to Camille Pleyel, thanks to whom he had money enough for the trip. There he composed as well a mazurka and a ballad.[118] As for Sand, whom "the little Chop"[119] liked to call "Jutrzenca" ("Aurora" in Polish), she was not idle. She looked after her lover "as though he were [her] child";[120] she bought, not without difficulty, everything the household needed; she would occasionally help out the cook and lend a hand to the local laundress, whose laziness she berated. She also schooled Maurice and Solange "six or seven hours" a day, and "as usual . . . spent half the night working on [her] own account."[121] So she became "father and mother to [her children], . . . the man who runs things outside the house and the woman who oversees things inside."[122] Already long used to writing at night while she was free from all the problems of life during the day, Sand finished up a revised version of *Lélia* and a new novel, *Spiridion*, whose hero is a young monk,[123] and which Gustave Doré illustrated with several drawings.

The health of Chopin, a "sweet and kind angel,"[124] was not improving, and Sand got really worried, even though he could still joke about it.[125] No doubt Maurice took advantage of his stay "in the south"[126] to get stronger, and Solange's disposition, "all resistance and rage," improved a bit, but the charterhouse was so damp, the hostility of the Majorcans so obvious, and Chopin's physical state so alarming that they decided to return to France at the end of February 1838. As Sand wrote in *A Winter in Majorca*, "We were . . . alone in Majorca, as alone as we would be in a desert, and when we had won our daily bread through a war with the *monkeys*, we would sit together as a family to laugh about it around the stove. But as the winter went on, sadness paralyzed my attempts to be jolly and serene. Our patient's health got steadily worse; the wind moaned in the ravine, rain battered at our windows, thunder penetrated our thick walls and threw its gloomy note in the midst of our laughter and children's games."[127] In a letter to Charlotte Marliani, Sand is even more brutal: "God forbid that I ever set foot in Spain again! The country doesn't suit me in any way, shape or form. . . . Majorca's climate was becoming more and more of a danger for Chopin; I hurried to get us out. We were like *pariahs* because of Chopin's cough and also because we didn't go to Mass. People threw rocks at my children on the road. They said we were *pagans*, what have you. It would take ten volumes to give you an idea ... of how mean that stupid, thieving, God-fearing race can be."[128]

In Marseilles a doctor named Cauvière examined Chopin and found him in critical condition. It was impossible to keep on traveling. "At night," Chopin wrote to Grzymala, "[George] works a lot. As for me, I sleep because I'm being given opium pills—and in the morning she sleeps and I stay put, cough, and meditate."[129] The musician's convalescence lasted four months. Maurice drew a portrait with the caption: "Chopin is scarcely having any fun in Marseilles, May 1839."[130]

During her stay in that "stupid city"[131] Sand composed a historical drama that took place centuries ago in Italy, where, for reasons of inheritance, the heroine was made to think she had been born a man and was reared as such. Published in 1840, *Gabriel* is one of Sand's most incisive works about sexual difference and its implications. There the author shows how strong prejudices against women are and, even though the demonstration remains a bit ambiguous, strives to convince her readers of their inanity. At the beginning of the play Gabriel declares to her tutor: "As for me, I don't feel my soul has a sex, as you're trying to prove. . . . I'm not absolutely brave, not absolutely fainthearted either. . . . Believe me, we're all subject to momentary impressions, and any man who would boast that he'd never been afraid would strike me as a great braggart. Likewise, I wouldn't be astonished to hear a woman say that on some days she is courageous."[132] Balzac said that he was "carried away" reading *Gabriel*. "It's a play by Shakespeare, and I don't understand why you haven't put it on stage,"[133] he wrote to Sand in June.

In early June, after a few days of vacation in Genoa, Chopin, Sand, and her children were back at Nohant. The summer of 1839 was peaceful. On the second floor of the house Chopin had a comfortable room with a view of the garden; his door was padded to protect him from outside noise. On a Pleyel grand piano in the formal living room he composed several important works, among which was the famous funeral march.[134] Sand admitted treating him like "another Maurice"[135] and trying to make the best of his unstable temperament and precarious health: "Chopin is always sometimes better, sometimes worse, never exactly sick or well. I really believe the poor child is doomed to being forever a bit languid. Fortunately, this doesn't drag down his state of mind. He is merry as soon as he feels a bit of energy, and when he's feeling melancholy, he takes to his piano and composes beautiful pages."[136] Plus, Sand was busy with the education of her children:

> I cannot teach Latin or Greek, but at least I've managed to teach French well, and we are up to our necks in history, philosophy, religion, with all the related questions of geography, literature, and art. In a word, Maurice [sixteen years old] and I are studying side by side, often consulting the encyclopedia [*New Encyclopedia*] of Leroux and Reynaud. . . . I vulgarize the text to make it easier to understand. . . . The rest of the time he is reading and drawing while I keep an eye on him. I do the same with Solange, adjusting the lessons to her mind and age [twelve years old]. . . . This tutoring is good for me, and I like it.[137]

From 1833 to 1837 Maurice had been studying at the Lycée Henri-IV, but Sand finally took him out because he was so unhappy there. After Jules Boucoiran and Félicien Mallefille, there were no more tutors. Sand herself would educate her son and then her daughter. But after Maurice, at age sixteen, went to study and work in Eugène Delacroix's studio in November 1839, she grew weary of the conflicts with Solange and decided to put her in a nonreligious boarding school in Paris. "I am very happy," she wrote to her old friend from Berry, Gustave Papet, ". . . [Maurice] is serious about painting and passionate about Delacroix. . . . Solange is still arrogant and a bit haughty, but she's also much better off. Boarding school suits her."[138]

Back in Paris in the fall of 1839, "after grousing, raging, fuming, and swearing at the upholsterers, the locksmiths, etc. etc., etc.,"[139] Sand moved to 16 rue Pigalle while Chopin kept his apartment at 5 rue Tronchet so that he could give lessons there. Balzac wrote to Ève Hanska:

G[eorge] Sand is living at 16 rue Pigalle, in a garden, . . . she has a dining room with sculpted oak furniture. Her little living room is the color of café au lait, and the formal living room is replete with superb Chinese vases full of flowers. There is always a planter loaded with flowers, the furniture is green, there is a sideboard with all kinds of curiosities, paintings by Delacroix, her portrait by Calamatta. . . . A magnificent piano, upright, square, in rosewood. Besides, Chopin is always there. *She smokes just CIG-ARETTES* and nothing else. She only gets up at four, by which time Chopin has finished giving his lessons. You get to her room by a series of steps called *miller's stairs*, going straight up and steep. Her bedroom is brown, her bed is two mattresses on the floor, *à la turque*. She has the pretty tiny, tiny hands of a child.[140]

Bit by bit Sand's life came to be entirely organized around Chopin. They spent the winter in Paris, the summer and a part of the fall at Nohant, where the children came to join them. Sand and Chopin entertained a lot, out in the country even more than in the city, his Polish friends, her friends and neighbors from Berry, in addition to Sand's socialist friends, with personalities as varied as Emmanuel Arago, a lawyer and vaudevillist, and Agricol Perdiguier, a carpenter from Avignon who had introduced Sand to *compagnonnage* or craftmen's associations. At Nohant: "We all dine outside, some friends or other come over, we smoke, chat, and when they've left in the evening, Chopin plays the piano for me as night falls, after which he falls asleep like a child at the same time as Maurice and Solange."[141]

Coddled "like a child," Sand's companion seems to have become physically aloof rather quickly from the woman to whom he was sincerely attached. All the while giving him a comfortable life, Chopin having no income aside from what he earned with his piano lessons and concerts, she put him in a context altogether new to him, that of a true family. It is quite enough to read Sand's letters[142] to understand that the musician was not easy to deal with. In Paris he would rage against the problems of being in a big city; in the country he often claimed to be bored, even though it was mainly there that he composed. Sand wrote: "My other son, Chopin, is still frail and sickly, . . . a perfect soul in an unsound body, consequently a restless imagination and an irresolute and melancholy disposition."[143]

Even though she would often make fun of an "atrabilious skeptic" and rail at Chopin's misanthropic whims and ways, Sand never hid her deep affection and boundless admiration for the exceptional talent of the man whom she called all kinds of inventive pet names in her correspondence. While Chopin was in Paris, she wrote to Albert Grzymala: "I miss him as much as he misses me. I need to keep an eye on him as much as he needs me to look after him. I miss his face, his voice, his piano, his sad little moods, and even the heartrending sound of his cough. . . . I'll never fail him, you can be sure, and my life is forever devoted to him."[144]

With the pianist Ignaz Moscheles, Chopin gave a recital for Louis-Philippe and his family at Saint-Cloud in October 1839. In 1841, after being out of the public eye for six years, he had a hard time making up his mind to give a concert at the Pleyel concert hall and then imposed such conditions that Sand wrote:

> A great, really great piece of news—the little Chip Chip is going to give a grrrrrreat concert. His friends have so stuffed his head with the idea that he let himself get talked into it . . . and there's nothing funnier than seeing the finicky, irresolute Chip forced not to change his mind anymore. . . . This chopinesque incubus will take place at the Salle Pleyel on the 26th [of April]. He doesn't want any posters, he doesn't want any programs, he doesn't want a big audience. He doesn't want people talking about it. He is afraid of so many things that I've told him to play without candles on a silent piano, and without anyone in the audience.[145]

The concert, for which Chopin played several of his own compositions,[146] was a great success: Franz Liszt wrote an enthusiastic review in the *Revue et Gazette Musicale* of 2 May. A few days later Sand wrote to Hippolyte Chatiron: "Chopin made it possible to loaf around all summer long by giving a concert where, in two hours and two brilliant executions, he pocketed some 6,000 francs plus a few hundred more amid shouts of *bravo, encore*, with the prettiest Parisiennes wildly stamping their feet."[147]

Chopin did a repeat performance the following year, with the same success,[148] and along with Pauline Viardot, the concert singer of international repute who was the daughter of the Spanish tenor Manuel Garcia, the sister of Maria Malibran, and one of the artists that Sand most admired and loved.[149]

In August 1842 Pauline and her husband, Louis Viardot, who directed the Théâtre-Italien made a long stay at Nohant. Maurice was then busy painting a copy of a portrait of Saint Anne by his master Delacroix that would wind up in the church of Nohant. Solange was out of school for the summer. They spent their days making music and, on Sand's advice, running around the countryside to listen to the chants and tunes of Berrichon folklore, the "solemn and melancholy chant this place's ancient tradition passes on . . . to the [plowmen],"[150] or the bourrées played on bagpipes and hurdy-gurdies to which people danced in the nearby villages. As Sand observed in *Consuelo*,

> There is music that one could call natural because it is not the product of science and reflection, but of an inspiration that escapes the grandeur of rules and conventions. That is folk music: of peasants in particular. What beautiful poems are born, live, and die among them, without ever having had the honor of being correctly noted. . . . The unknown artist who improvises his rustic ballad while watching his sheep or pushing his plow . . . will have a hard time remembering his fleeting thoughts precisely. . . . That's why these pastoral songs and ballads get lost for the most part. . . . The musicians who know the rules of music don't bother to collect them.[151]

In the fall of 1843 Sand and Chopin moved from the rue Pigalle to 5 and 7 square d'Orléans. Maurice and Solange had rooms there as well. As Sand recalled in *Story of My Life*,

The kind and active Marliani [the wife of the Spanish consul] had arranged our family life. . . . We had dinner at her place all together, sharing the cost. It was a fine association, a bargain like all associations, and it allowed me to see lots of people at Madame Marliani's house, my friends more privately at my place, and to get to work when I felt like being alone. Chopin too was delighted to have a lovely, secluded living room where he could go compose or dream. . . . Maurice had his own rooms and his studio on the floor above me. Near me Solange had a pretty little room where she loved to act like a *lady* . . . on the days when she was free to leave [her boarding school].[152]

For three years Sand and Chopin went back and forth between Paris and Nohant. What beautiful summers when music and literature were in constant dialogue! Under Sand's guidance, "Chopin who *runs from* success, Solange the quibbler, Bouli [Maurice] the child of nature,"[153] Pauline and Louis Viardot, who soon had a little girl, and with them Sand's childhood friends from Berry would spend hours eating, swimming in the Indre, amusing themselves with a few memorable pranks, for example, Sand's maid-servant passing herself off as her mistress for some unwelcome visitors,[154] or the imitations done by Chopin, who would mimic friends they had in common, musicians he knew, or even certain typically Polish characters.[155] In addition to long walks through the Vallée-Noire, they also made a few short trips, on horseback or by carriage, to Gargilesse, Crozant, Chateaubrun, Dun-le-Palestel, Éguzon, or the ruins of the abbey of Fontgombault. Sand would sometimes read excerpts from the novels she was writing or Chopin would sit down at the piano. At night, when the house fell silent, she would go on writing for hours on loose-leaf paper or in notebooks of her own making.

There was painting as well. Eugène Delacroix, "the greatest painter of the time,"[156] who had been friends with Sand since painting his first portrait of her in 1833, would come down to see the "artists" in Berry. After having done the magnificent portraits of Sand and Chopin in 1838,[157] a few pastels and pencil drawings, including one of Maurice lying on his belly and drawing, Delacroix painted a corner of the garden, and subsequently, on a canvas slip belonging to the mistress of the house, an *Education of the Virgin* at Nohant in 1842. He returned the following summer, in 1843, and did, in particular, studies of flowers.[158]

At Nohant, "a rustic nest where all the ranks are not yet mixed up enough for my own taste, and from which the prevailing *social virtues* are banished,"[159] Sand's old dream came true for a moment, the dream of a community of artists drawn together in every possible way, through taste, temperament, and political convictions, and living out of a common purse, as they had at the square d'Orléans.

Consuelo most clearly springs from this passionate desire. The novel also illustrates an exceptional sensitivity to song and voice, plus a rare knowledge of music and its vocal repertory. Composed of memories and dreams, powerfully informed by meditations on philosophy and religion, music and politics, this masterpiece began appearing in installments in February 1842. It was dedicated to Pauline Viardot, "my dear Consuelo,"[160] who directly inspired this portrait of a female artistic genius. *Consuelo* and its sequel, *The Countess von Rudolstadt* [*La comtesse de Rudolstadt*], take place between 1742 and 1755 in Enlightenment Europe. The heroine is a girl of humble origins, "with good Spanish blood,"[161] whose exceptional musical gifts lead to a career as an opera singer. Written in four parts, the novel's fresco begins in Venice, where Consuelo sings Pergolesi's *Salve Regina*, and continues at the castle of the Giants in Bohemia where Albert von Rudolstadt, an inspired madman, falls in love with her; it also takes byways to Vienna, then to Berlin and Prague. After thousands of adventures, Consuelo finally meets up once again with Albert von Rudolstadt, who has never ceased to feel infinite love for her.

Music is everywhere in the novel. People sing, are moved by the admirable voices of a few great artists of the time, compare the creations of the most famous composers, and the young Haydn has a brief role as the young woman's mischievous traveling companion. At the end, with her husband and two children, Consuelo decides to go back out on the road: "Life is a voyage with life as its goal,"[162] the narrative voice concludes on an optimistic note. "What talent, Christ almighty! what talent! that's what I shout out, every now and then,"[163] Flaubert wrote, rereading the novel in December 1866.

In May 1846, when Chopin left for Nohant in order to finish up a few compositions, the tensions multiplied. For quite some time Sand had felt deeply disappointed by this romance, which had gradually become a heavy chain for her.[164] To Albert Grzymala, in whom she had confided about her relationship with Chopin from the start, she wrote: "The disease gnawing at this poor creature's mind and body has been killing me for a long time, and I see him going away without ever having been able to do him any good, since it is his restless, jealous, and testy love for me that is the main reason for his sadness. Seven years long I've lived like a virgin with him and *the others*. I've grown old prematurely, and even without any effort or sacrifice, since I was so weary of passion and incurably disillusioned."[165]

The attitude of Sand's children further complicated a situation they had known since childhood. Now twenty-two, Maurice meant to be the master of Nohant and scarcely tolerated Chopin's (timid) interference in this matter. Solange, who was eighteen, had an ambiguous relationship with her mother's companion: Chopin was obviously charmed by the girl whom her mother considered lazy and vindictive, as the letters addressed to her as "fatty" or "Mademoiselle Margot" had long demonstrated. Sand had asked Chopin to moderate his "exclusive and jealous passion"[166] for her, to send away his Polish servant and to stop entertaining a few indelicate Polish guests at Nohant. Her socialist friends, worker-poets, *compagnons* or members of craftsmen's associations, and various sympathizers were not Chopin's favorites. Delacroix also complained about them.

The publication, in March 1846, of *Lucrezia Floriani* did not help matters. As she would do elsewhere, Sand created a kind of auto-fiction where it is not hard to recognize a few members of her entourage. Weak and whimsical, Prince Karol who pursues the actress Lucrezia with his jealous love naturally brings Chopin to mind. Yet one has to believe Sand when, defending herself in *Story of My Life* for drawing (only) the portrait of Chopin, she asserts: "Nature does not draw the way art does, however realist it may be."[167]

When Chopin left Nohant at the end of the summer, his relationship with Sand was at the point of death. In Paris he saw his students and musician friends with pleasure, including the cellist Auguste Franchomme for whom he composed a few uncommonly beautiful pieces for cello and piano. He met Jane Stirling, who would be his muse for the last three years of his life.

Solange soon fell in love with a local squire from Berry, Fernand de Preaulx, and there was talk of marriage. In February 1847 Sand and her daughter posed in the Paris studio of the sculptor Auguste Clésinger, who, at the age of thirty-three, was enjoying a solid reputation. He made a quite beautiful bust of Sand and a molding of her arm, both of which are now at the Musée de la vie romantique in Paris. Solange fell in love with Clésinger, broke up with Preaulx in despair,[168] and decided to marry the artist despite warnings from her mother and the unsavory information Sand had gathered about him. "Instead of a modest and sweet marriage, [Solange] has chosen a brilliant and scorching one,"[169] remarked Sand, who feared that "pride plays a bigger role in her life than tenderness and devotion."[170] Yet to Maurice she confessed that Clésinger's resoluteness, "that intense willpower, indefatigable and unfailing, astonishes and greatly pleases [me]."[171]

The wedding was celebrated at Nohant on 19 May, with the bride's father present. Sand gave her daughter a generous dowry as well as the elegant Parisian house known as l'hôtel de Narbonne, 89 rue de la Harpe, where the young couple would live.[172] Chopin did not attend the ceremony, but he supported Solange against her mother, despite his dislike for the sculptor. In July he wrote Sand a letter (destroyed) in which he criticized her attitude toward Solange and said he wanted to distance himself from Sand. She made a brief reply, expressing her astonishment at "this bizarre end to nine years of exclusive affection."[173]

In the course of a short visit to Nohant from Solange and her husband in July 1847, a violent scene erupted. "A joker like Dumas, and like him deep in debt,"[174] Clésinger proposed that his mother-in-law take out a mortgage on Nohant and give him some 24,000 francs that he needed to pay off debts. When she protested, he accused her of having made him think she was richer than she actually was and wound up threatening her with a gun. Maurice intervened when Clésinger punched her right in the chest. The priest and the painter Eugène Lambert, one of Maurice's friends, also got in the act and tried to calm the sculptor down: "Can you imagine such scenes at Nohant, in my family, with my temper-ament, and those of Maurice, Augustine, and Lambert? in front of the priest, and with some of the servants forced to step in?"[175] Sand asked one of her correspondents. The break was definitive; the couple left Nohant, never to return.

It was a big shock. Sand found herself alone, once and for all separated from Chopin and at odds with a daughter whom she found most ungrateful. Plus, the wedding plans of her second cousin, Augustine Brault, came to an abrupt halt. Sand had got it into her head that she should marry first Maurice, then the painter Théodore Rousseau, who spending a few days at Nohant had painted something on this motif.[176] When this plan came to naught, Sand blamed her daughter's little schemes.[177] "This year 1847," she wrote to Guiseppe Mazzini, "[may be] the most troubled and painful in my whole life."[178]

In a very long letter to Emmanuel Arago she retraced the his-tory of her difficult relationship with her daughter, detailed the dreadful scene that had just taken place, and marveled at Chopin's unfailing support of Solange, even though she had precipitated their breakup: "I know I was . . . the tenderest, the weakest, and the most good-natured [of mothers]. I worked like a slave to sat-isfy a taste for luxury that was certainly not mine. . . . I yielded to everything; I was her lady's maid, her seamstress, her jockey, her hairdresser, her walking companion, going out, coming back in, staying home, paying, sewing, working day and night, being a slave to her whims, and never knowing how to refuse or punish." Then, with regard to Chopin, she declared: "For me, good riddance! the chain is broken! Never succumbing to his narrow-minded and despotic spirit, but always chained by my pity and the fear of making him die of heartache, for nine long years I was brimming with life and bound to a cadaver."[179] To which Emmanuel Arago replied: "Solange really only loves herself; she sees things just in relation to herself, and wants nothing more than seeing everything going out from her and coming back to her. . . . For several years Chopin found her fascinating and gladly put up with things from her that would have exasperated him from anybody else. I saw, saw, really saw, that he had deep feelings for her. . . . What should you do? Nothing—What should you say? It's bad for him, much more so than for you.—The chain was weighing on you: now it's no more."[180] A year later, in March 1848, Sand ran into Chopin by accident, in the stairs to Charlotte Marliani's apartment. He told her about the birth of little Jeanne Clésinger, who would die a few days later. Sand did not know a thing about it.

After a harrowing concert tour in England in the spring of 1849 Chopin died in Paris on 17 October from tuberculosis, a disease from which he had suffered his whole life long. Auguste Clésinger made his death mask and took a molding of his hand, both of which are at the Musée de la vie romantique. Thanks to a collection organized by Delacroix, Solange's husband also sculpted Chopin's funerary monument at the Père-Lachaise cemetery. As Sand wrote to Pierre-Jules Hetzel, "This death has affected me deeply. . . . Up there or down in that other place . . . , he'll remember that for nine years I looked after him better than most people look after their own son; that I sacrificed some excellent and honest relationships to his jealousy, his whims; that my heart suffered for loving him, during these nine years. . . . After which I no longer want anything to do with that bitter life full of duplicity, ingratitude, and revolting injustice."[181]

Later on, in *Story of My Life*, Sand would draw a much more nuanced portrait of Chopin; the memory of the musician who was "modest by principle and sweet by habit, but . . . imperious by instinct and full of legitimate pride"[182] opens and closes this great narrative of the self that she began writing in 1847. There she evokes "years of tenderness, trust, and gratitude that one hour of injustice or turmoil has not canceled out."[183] In a text dated 1841

Sand found just the right words for Chopin's exceptional talent as a performer and his genius as a composer: "And then the blue note sounds, and we are in the azure of a transparent night. . . . A sublime song rises in the air. The master knows just what he is doing. . . . He knows that music is a human impression and a human manifestation. It is a human soul thinking, a human voice expressing itself. It is man in the presence of his emotions, translating them by the feeling they inspire."[184]

COMBAT

Marked by Sand's relationship with Chopin and her friendship with the opera singer Pauline Viardot, the 1840s put music at the heart of Sand's life more clearly than at any other time. These were also years of combat that made Sand a true militant, and outside of this context her novels can be only superficially understood.

In her writing Sand continued to express convictions directly inspired by Pierre Leroux, who was still her mentor—she dedicated *Spiridion* to him[185]—and by a resolutely social Catholicism. As *Consuelo* and many other Sand novels of the period bear witness, her political vocabulary remained deeply marked by a religious vision. "The voice of the people is the voice of God,"[186] proclaimed Leroux in one of his slogans much appreciated by Christian Romanticism to which Victor Hugo and Lamartine adhered as well.

Why did Sand never stop pleading for different political principles, a different form of government, a different society? First of all, an element of personal history, of which she was terribly proud: "As for me, there's no bourgeois blood in my veins. I am the daughter of a patrician man and a Bohemian woman. . . . I'll stand with the slave and the Bohemian woman, and not with kings and their henchmen."[187] She had a "great *love for all humanity*," then a "feeling of human fraternity," "the dream of a better society"[188] for those whom she would henceforth call "the proletarians," peasants, artisans, and workers, men and women. The words say it: while for Sand politics was reflection and strategy, that is, "ideology" in the wake of Rousseau and all those whom Pierre Leroux rallied around "socialism," a term of his own invention, it is also affection, sympathy, compassion. Its guiding *ideal* was an old dream shared by the children of the Revolution, meaning equality hand in hand with fraternity.

More and more preoccupied with independence and freedom of expression, Sand would found a literary review and help create an opposition newspaper in Berry. The press had begun to play a considerable role in people's lives. When Émile de Girardin established *La Presse* in 1836, the first penny press daily, France was once and for all plunged into the era of mass media. The role that newspapers, big or "little," played in spreading information and ideas kept growing and growing. Sand knew this, since she had cut her teeth on a little satirical paper and published most of her novels in installments in newspapers and magazines.

Her relationship with the director of the *Revue des Deux Mondes* had been steadily running out of steam for some time. The reasons for this were directly related to Sand's openly socialist politics, which François Buloz did not care to endorse in the *Revue* under his management. During the summer of 1841, as was her habit, Sand gave Buloz the manuscript of her new novel *Horace*. It took place in Paris at the beginning of the July Monarchy, with a few workers and students criticizing the government, deploring the massacre that had taken place in the rue du Cloître Saint-Méry, and calling for resistance. "Given the state of the nation and the work of secret societies, it would be unwise and perhaps culpable to throw the restive masses something so easy to exploit,"[189] Buloz wrote to Sand. He proposed changes to the manuscript, which was nothing out of the ordinary, but he also suggested cutting certain passages. At first Sand could not believe it, and then she got furious. "I do not want to change it. No, a hundred times **NO**,"[190] she replied. Soon she severed her contract with the *Revue des Deux Mondes* and broke off all dealing with Buloz.

From this falling-out there emerged a project: creating a literary review less sympathetic to the Parisian intelligentsia and the government, freer in tone, and more open to social questions. To this end Sand first assessed her financial situation, then made contact with a few loyal friends, and wound up finding the necessary funds. Pierre Leroux, Louis Viardot, and Sand, "in agreement on everything as though we were one,"[191] would be the directors. "This time finally, . . . I can unburden myself with the hope of being heard and not being a lone voice amid society's hullabaloo,"[192] she wrote to Scipion du Roure. The first issue of *La Revue Indépendante* appeared in November 1841, and it contained the first chapter of the novel that Buloz had refused, plus an article on proletarian poetry that Sand signed with the name of Blaise Bonnin, a fictional peasant from Berry who would make several other appearances later on.

Proletarian poetry had been encouraged by the recent creation of journals such as *La Ruche Populaire*, *L'Union*, or *L'Atelier*. There men and women of humble origins published their poems and requested the patronage of men of letters of the time. The latter would advise them, help them find publishers, and sometimes write a preface to their works. Sand admired the poems of Charles Poncy, a bricklayer from Toulon with whom she would remain friends for the rest of her life, and she agreed to preface his publications. She also supported artisans and workers with the names Gilland, Magu, Reboul, Vinçart, and Adélaïde Bousquet. Her admiration for proletarian poetry fortified her views on the "naturally" poetic nature of "proletarians" and the "primitive" dimension of their talent. She asserted in her article on the subject: "*Hégésippe Moreau* . . . and many others have taught us that the people, the proletarians, have every kind of talent, all sorts of genius. How fortunate this country would be if it knew how to stimulate the greatest possible issue from all its children, according to the natural gifts of each and every one."[193]

The case of Agricol Perdiguier, a carpenter from Avignon, *compagnon du Devoir* and the author of the *Livre du compagnonnage* [*Book of Craftsmen's Guilds*] published in 1839, is not the same. With him Sand learned how craftsmen's associations worked, and about their history and traditions. Her taste for secret societies, the Illuminati, the Freemasons, and the Carbonari, was rekindled. This inspired her to write the *Companion of the Tour de France* [*Compagnon du tour de France*], which appeared in 1840. With her hero, the carpenter Pierre Huguenin, who is in love with Yseult de Villepreux, she drew for the first time a worker's portrait in a novel and declared in the preface: "A worker is a man just like any other . . . , and I'm really astonished this still astonishes some people. You don't have to have the *baccalaureat* [national diploma required for entering the French university system] to know as much as everybody else with the diploma. . . . This so-called inferiority of race or sex is a prejudice that today doesn't even benefit from the excuse of sincerity."[194] The novel did not get good reviews. Proponents of laissez-faire economics and supporters of Bonaparte criticized its didactic dimension and ideological biases, while Marie d'Agoult wrote an acidic review in *La Presse*. *Horace*, Sand's next novel, did not fare any better, which made Balzac write, with a lot of exaggeration: "Nobody at all wants anything more by G[eorge] Sand since her last productions have come out. . . . *The Companion of the Tour of France* has been her death."[195]

The first number of *La Revue Indépendante* was a great success, and at the end of 1841 Sand wrote to Théodore de Seynes: "My role as editor and also Leroux's focus on the intellectual and spiritual side of things, but since this review has in the end been created by our feelings and opinions, we want it and our ideas to succeed. . . . I think we'll manage to do something conscientious and serious that will bear fruit. My novels will only be the hype to pull in the idle strollers . . . , they'll keep things going, and the primary goal of the review, which is to speak freely and openly to sympathetic souls, will be achieved if God is willing . Up to now the machine is running fine, and there are tons of subscribers."[196]

The second thing on Sand's agenda was to get an opposition newspaper going. This project was set in motion by a case that in July 1843 signaled her first political move, strictly speaking. A feeble-minded girl of fifteen in the care of the nuns of La Châtre had been deliberately abandoned out in the countryside; after wandering around for several weeks and falling victim to vagabonds, she was finally found, and it was clear that she was pregnant. Sand decided to lodge a protest straightaway in *La Revue Indépendante*, first, by writing an article signed Blaise Bonnin, accusing the Mother Superior of the institution where Fanchette had been placed as well as the administration that had covered for her; second, by publishing a short statement signed with her own name this time, in which she denounced the failings of the administration at all levels. Finally, Sand placed these texts in a brochure and put it on sale, with all the profits going to the girl's benefit.

Despite a swell of opinion in Fanchette's favor, the crown prosecutor of La Châtre lifted all sanctions against the religious institution. Plus, in a letter that he asked *La Revue Indépendante* to publish, he accused Sand of turning the affair into a novel. She replied in no uncertain terms: "If Fanchette, already feeble-minded, has not gone mad . . . , if she is infected with the shameful wounds of debauchery and prostitution, whose fault is it? And *there are no guilty parties?* and *your finding that there were no grounds for prosecution* in this *deplorable* event is not *clear proof* to the contrary? . . . and I've been making a novel out of this? Ah! then you're doing the same thing yourself! if that's a reason for shame, drink it down."[197] During the Fanchette affair which she would recall in her novel *Jeanne*, published in 1844,[198] Sand saw how difficult it was to express her ideas and to get them in print except through her own review. "Events of the same kind," she observed, "and even more dreadful, are often repeated right in front of our eyes . . . , without . . . public indignation finding a means of complaint."[199] Convinced that Berry needed an opposition newspaper, she started collecting funds, finding collaborators, setting up a board of directors, and convincing a trustworthy printer to join in; she wound up accepting the help of Pierre Leroux and his brother, who were working as printers in nearby Boussac. Sand had perfectly clear ideas about what she wanted to do: "[I] love journalism, especially the provincial sort. There's more loyalty, more independence, more of a future in it. . . . This mustn't be Mr. So and So's paper, even less George Sand's. . . . It has to be the chorus of the sacred battalion, and that those who only read the paper participate in its philosophy just as much as those who write it; we'll make a proclamation of all this at the start, using all the right words."[200]

It was a done deal by 1 September 1844, when there appeared the first number of *L'Éclaireur, Journal des Départements de l'Indre, du Cher et de la Creuse*, printed at La Châtre, with the republican journalist Victor Borie as editor in chief. Two thousand francs per year were put to use for a weekly paper with twenty-five shareholders. The paper bluntly stated that it was created in opposition "to our local authorities who are now possessed of . . . revolting insolence and immorality."[201] In the third number Sand wrote an open letter "To the Founders of *L'Éclaireur de l'Indre*" in which she defined the relationship she meant to have with the paper and reaffirmed her faith in a society "founded on principles very different from those now governing society."[202] The Revolution of 1848 would be the end of *L'Éclaireur*, its last number appearing in July. *La Revue Indépendante* met the same fate.

From this point on Sand had two forums of very different kinds for expressing her ideas. Literature and politics combined perfectly in her mind, and she was eager to put her talent and fame as an author to work in order to realize a passionate hope, the "dream of a better society,"[203] with all it implied. Sand had a keen sense of history, with a vivid perception of the *moment* when change might become possible, plus a remarkable understanding that it takes time for mentalities to evolve. Since mentalities curb change rather than encouraging it, one could not, she thought, try to force fate at all costs. Often bold political moves grind to a sudden halt because the people who undertook them had misjudged people's state of mind. While awaiting some rare conjuncture that might allow major changes to take place, one must still work to reform everything limiting the rights, too scarce, of some and promoting the power, too great, of others. In the article entitled "La politique et le socialisme"[204] she wrote: "We agree to call *politics* an entirely material action exercised by society to modify and improve its institutions; *socialism*, an entirely scientific action exercised on people so that they want to reform social institutions."

Before the Revolution of 1848 Sand multiplied her support for all criticism of the existing government; she called for "democracy,"[205] demanding respect and consideration for the proletarians, the life force of the nation, and most particularly for the peasants. Sand was one of the only writers of her generation who really knew the "milieu" that made up the greatest part of the population of France. It is quite enough to compare Balzac's *The Peasants* [*Les paysans*] with Sand's *The Master Pipers* [*The maîtres sonneurs*] to see everything separating a writer who tends to see peasants as nothing more than ignorant schemers and one who takes an interest in all the players on the rural scene, their habits and customs, their way of living and thinking.

Blaise Bonnin had defended Fanchette in *La Revue Indépendante*. He would reappear in *L'Éclaireur* to explain why the peasants lived in such wretched conditions:

> I don't know how it started, but with the Empire, the Restoration, and even more with the recent Revolution of 1830, feudalism, the tithe, serfdom, and even the corvée . . . , all that fell back on us. . . . Feudalism is the absolute power of the "haves" over the "have-nots." Taxes are only for the benefit of the rich. . . . Serfdom is the state of our wretched lives, and it puts us at the mercy of the bourgeois usurer, the bourgeois farmer, the bourgeois or nonbourgeois proprietor; and the corvée is service in kind for the so-called public good![206]

Formulated in "simple" words, Bonnin's words indict daily hardships, governmental measures without any real effect, and the urgent need for education at the lowest levels of society. At the same time Sand was actively campaigning for "the nearly free distribution of good books,"[207] a project that would be fine-tuned several times without ever amounting to anything.

Were her readers fooled by this voice in male disguise and the new pseudonym of Blaise Bonnin? In *L'Éclaireur de l'Indre* Sand took care to specify: "The pseudonym concealing someone's sex is no mystery for anyone who has paid some attention to what we've written. We do not acknowledge some innate superiority in the other sex; but we certainly have to acknowledge the consequences of the incomplete education we've received. . . . Nothing replaces, in the life of women, that fundamental education, that *Minerva armed to the teeth* that Diderot says springs out of the young high school graduate's brain to combat his first impressions, his first errors."[208] And she added: "In our eyes, the cause of women and the cause of the people are strikingly similar, and that seems to make them stand together in solidarity."[209]

Sand was not the only one to imagine a "natural" alliance between those whom society ignored, exploited, and mistreated. The Saint-Simonians thought the same thing, as well as a few others associated with 1840s socialism, Flora Tristan, for example. She connected with Sand in 1844 while starting her tour of France in hopes of creating the "workers' union" she so wanted to see. In the midst of her travels she would die of exhaustion in Bordeaux. "She is an active woman, courageous, I think sincere, but brimming with pride and confidence in the infallibility of her socialist discoveries that are just childish nonsense,"[210] Sand noted to one of her correspondents, regretting that the author of the *Peregrinations of a pariah* [*Pérégrinations d'une paria*] thought she had a monopoly on defending the "proletarian classes."[211] In the same period Sand was briefly in touch with Pauline Roland, a feminist socialist who collaborated on Pierre Leroux's *Revue Sociale* and who would be deported to Algeria after the coup d'état of 1851.[212]

During these intellectually and politically productive years Sand did not stop turning out novels, far from it. She often said it was her *nature* to write novels and tell stories for fun, but not any old way, not just to entertain herself and her readers. The "mission" of the writer, whom Victor Hugo saw as a prophet, a visionary leading and enlightening the people, was to make all kinds of literature into a forum for expressing thoughts about society, its history and workings, and also about what would be needed to transform society.

Sand's novels are resolutely utopian, especially in this period. Stemming from her political convictions and not from some taste for fantasy and science fiction, this dimension of her work is based on careful observation of reality, without which there is no political thought. Consequently, there is no vague idealism, irrepressible naiveté, or nonchalant sentimentality in her novels, as some would later charge. Her objectives are clearly defined, her ambitions precisely laid out, and her reasons explained a hundred times over. All this is combined with a great narrative mastery, with its rebounds, pauses, surprises, and a gallery of "typical" characters—except that there is always a very well-educated young woman and a young man who is sensitive to the temperament of the woman who seems like his equal right from the start. This blending of utopian thought and realism gives her novels a particular intensity that resonates with the novels of Victor Hugo, Eugène Sue, Alphonse de Lamartine, or Alexandre Dumas fils when they tackle the "social question" and work it into their fiction.

In January 1845, *The Miller at Angibault* [*Le meunier d'Angibault*] started appearing, despite various problems,[213] in installments in *La Réforme*. Set in the Vallée-Noire, this work is reminiscent of *Valentine* and foreshadows the rustic novels. Through the conversations of Marcelle, an enlightened female aristocrat, Henri, a very well-educated manual laborer from Paris, and Master Louis, a wise and sensible miller, Sand condemns the prejudices linked to sex and social status. At the end, a utopian order has been achieved: the rich and the poor unite, the family comes back together and grows like a community; the evil ones, selfish aristocrats and greedy peasants, are punished. At the same time Sand delivers an excellent analysis of country ways, rural living conditions, the economic problems facing the miller as well as the peasants on whom his business depends.

She does much the same the following year with *The Devil's Pool*, conceived and written prodigiously fast: "I've finished my little novel, I did it in four days. . . . I did it a hundred times faster than I thought I could. *It just came*,"[214] she announced to Anténor Joy, who was in charge of serials at the newspaper *L'Époque*. Dedicated to Frédéric Chopin, *The Devil's Pool* recounts the love between two young peasants from Berry, Germain and Marie, who one night get lost in the woods and camp out at a spot known as "the Devil's pool." A hemp-beater tells their story at an evening gathering, just as Sand remembered from her childhood: "When the hemp-beaters came to crush [the hemp], . . . half the village wanted to listen to their stories, so they were given a place near the little door of the courtyard looking out on the square."[215] Sand used this model for various reasons: aesthetic—to invent a new style and a new form, political—to preach sexual and class equality, and ethical—to promote kindness and generosity.

The language of the tale is plain, full of imagery, dotted with Berrichon dialect. Through these efforts of style whose simplicity masks truly great creativity, Sand meant to "translate" the "ancient and artless language of peasants from these parts."[216] *The Devil's Pool* also stems from meditation on folk art and the natural artistic bent of peasants, most clearly expressed in their tales, songs and legends, dances and costumes. In the author's apostrophe to the reader at the beginning of the tale, Sand redefines her poetics:

> Certain artists of our day . . . try their best to depict pain, abject poverty, Lazarus's dung heap. This can be part of art and philosophy; but, by depicting poverty in such an ugly, debased way . . . have they reached their goal, and is the effect salutary, as they would wish it to be?
>
> We believe that art has a mission of feeling and love, that today's novel ought to replace the parable and fable of primitive times. . . . Art is not a study of positive reality; it is a search for ideal truth.[217]

Once Germain and Marie are married, the novel returns to everyday life, ending with a description of the three-day celebrations that weddings in Berry used to be, an ethnographic approach indicating that period's interest in such matters.[218]

There follows in 1847 *Monsieur Antoine's Sin* [*Le péché de monsieur Antoine*], which in part reproduces the basic outline of *The Miller of Angibault*, where a young socialist falls in love with an aristocrat, but this time Sand expands her plea for profound reforms from society's top to bottom. Thus, the hero, Émile Cardonnet, in conversation with M. de Boisguibault, attacks "aristocracy as well as money, big property-owners, the power of individuals, the slavery of the masses, Jesuitical Catholicism, so-called divine right, the inequality of rights and privileges, the base of constituted society, man's domination of woman, considered a piece of merchandise in the marriage contract and a piece of property in the contract of public morality."[219]

The following year these questions would be more than ever in the news.

"A SORT OF STATESMAN"[220]

Who was George Sand at the beginning of 1848? A public figure, admired by some and harshly criticized by others for having joined forces with the "visionaries," the socialists and republicans, and without making any secret about it. Sand had not only teamed up with them, but, thanks to the creation of *La Revue Indépendante* and then *L'Éclaireur de l'Indre*, she was one of their most active and effective advocates. She did not just keep up with what was happening on the social front, but also wrote novels where her characters discussed political concerns close to her heart. But let there be no mistake. Referring to *Monsieur Antoine's Sin*, she observed to Jean Dessoliaire, a tailor and republican activist: "I've tried to bring up some serious problems in texts where the frivolous, altogether fantastical form lets the imagination go in search of an absolute ideal without any political drawbacks. . . . The characters just talk on and on, and nothing really matters, it's like people chatting in front of the fireplace, trying to reckon with the present and the future."[221] Even if it is clear that her political activity influenced her literary career and that her convictions can be found, at least partially, in the words of her characters, Sand still did not confuse the two activities and considered them quite distinct: "A novel is not a treaty,"[222] she concluded.

In 1848, "Madame Sand," as she was often referred to, was a forty-four-year-old woman with a penetrating gaze, forthright manners, and resolutely simple dress. She had been separated from her companion Chopin for a year and was living alone at Nohant with her son, who would soon turn twenty-five. He shared her political views and intellectual interests, and she often said he was her reason for life.[223] Sand was also the mother of a twenty-one-year-old daughter who had married a few months earlier, and from whom she was estranged after a conflict that would never be resolved. As for her private life, she had not concealed from her friends how disillusioned, sad, and deeply discouraged she felt. The joyous optimism that reigns in most of her novels, the declarations of feeling as well as the call for a life that makes sense because of a strong, faithful, and definitive love, the depictions of family as an open association based on the model of the Fourierist phalanstery, where generations and social classes harmoniously mix together, all this had to seem like some fantastic notion, really quite far removed from her own existence. "Love and I haven't been passing through the same gate for quite a while,"[224] she wrote to Emmanuel Arago in 1846.

The Revolution of 1848 has generated stories, personal accounts, and analyses galore. To have a precise view of a politically complex moment in which Sand was, for a few months in Paris, one of the privileged actors, one has to go back in history. A very active opposition made up of liberals, Bonapartists, republicans, and socialists wanted this revolution that was precipitated by economic crisis. Discontent with a "citizen-king" and the way he was governing the country had been simmering for years. These feelings had been fanned by a particularly dynamic press opposed to Louis-Philippe, and satirical newspapers constantly undermined the authority of "the pear"[225] with tons of caricatures of the king and his ministers.

"Someone imagines an ideal; people laugh and forgive him, saying: it's beautiful, too beautiful. Then time marches on, things happen, and the ideal goes out of fashion,"[226] Sand had written to Charles Poncy, the worker-poet whom she had taken under her wing. Then, at the end of February, all of a sudden, the famous ideal seemed about to become reality. After a few days of insurrection, barricades, and riots in Paris, Louis-Philippe abdicated. On 24 February the Second Republic was proclaimed, and a provisional government was set in place while a general election was being organized. Several reforms were announced right away: the death penalty for political crimes, slavery, censorship, and debtors' prisons, these were all abolished. There would be universal suffrage—for men.

On 1 March Sand arrived in Paris and moved into a little apartment at 8 rue de Condé, right near the Palace of Luxembourg. There she saw her republican and socialist friends, among them, Louis Blanc, Jean Reynaud, Étienne Arago, and Armand Barbès. The year before, while he was painting the ceiling of the library of the Palace of Luxembourg, Delacroix in his gallery of historical character had modeled Aspasia on Sand. A lovely nod to his artistic friend, a little prophetic sign.

Sand soon had a pass from Ledru-Rollin giving her access to all the members of the government. On 4 March, pleased to see the calm reigning over the funerals for the victims of the recent riots, she summed things up for her cousin René de Villeneuve:

> There's no reason to regret what we got rid of. Now we're leaping into the unknown with faith and hope. . . . This republic will not repeat the mistakes and aberrations of the republic you knew [in 1793]. No party has that in mind. The proletarians have been sublimely courageous and gentle. The government is *for the most part* made up of pure and honest men. I went to make sure of that with my own eyes, since I'm closely associated with several of them. . . . We owe them [the proletarians] for not having let bloody battles go on and on, and the wealthy owe them for having inspired trust and calm in the poor. . . . Don't stop loving me, even though I'm a *republican*.[227]

To her correspondents Sand hailed the advent of the "true republic"[228] with enthusiasm, saying again and again that she totally identified with the masses starting on their way to democracy. A few days later she was back in Nohant. Maurice had just been elected mayor of the little town of Nohant-Vicq, a position that he would keep for just a few months, and Sand was eager to check that the electoral lists of the department of Indre had at least one candidate who was a worker and another who was a peasant. "This is a difficult pill to swallow for the bourgeoisie," she noted, "and yet it's not much at all for the proletarians."[229] She wanted to make sure that people in the countryside did not dismiss the sudden change of regime as some Parisian scheme with which they could not identify and that would be of no benefit to them. This was a tough task, and Sand knew it. Peasants in Berry were naturally suspicious, and the people with power had no intention of sharing it.

Yet Sand's positions were hardly of a sort to reassure moderates. Even if she took care to clarify in private that "the kind of communism preached up until now is not [mine],"[230] the term had the same meaning for her as it did for the radical Left. Although she wrote in a text addressed "To the Wealthy" that she did not want to see conservatives waving the word around like a scarecrow, she still maintained that France "was called to be [communist] within a hundred years,"[231] meaning perfectly egalitarian, and endowed with a form of government where all the social forces would work together in association.[232]

She also published several calls to the proletarians, inviting them to be courageous, determined, politically aware, and also to cast their votes: "The present, oh proletarians! you've found it: it's the public forum, it's liberty; it's the republican form of government that must be maintained at all costs; it's the right to think, to speak, to write; it's the right to vote and to elect representatives, the source of all the other rights . . . ; it's the right to live; it's the only way of quickly working toward . . . the miracle of fraternal union that will destroy every false distinction and eliminate the very word of *class* from the book of a new and different humanity."[233]

At the Ministry of Public Instruction Jean Reynaud got her a job writing pamphlets for the masses. The character of Blaise Bonnin was once again enlisted to spread ideas whose force resulted from their "simple" formulation. Speaking in the voice of a Berrichon peasant, Sand called for determination, but without impatience, and respect for the rules of democracy; she reminded everybody that the workers in Paris and the peasants were "two men with the same blood and the same heart"[234] and that the capital of France could do nothing without support from the provinces.[235] She was also entrusted with writing editorials for the official newspaper of the provisional government, the *Bulletin de la République*. For several weeks Sand contributed actively, albeit anonymously, to the *Bulletin*. "Here I am . . . doing the work of a statesman," she wrote to Maurice. "I've already written two government circulars today, one for the Ministry of Public Instruction, and one for the Ministry of Internal Affairs."[236] She added: "What's funny is that all this is addressed to *mayors*, and you're going to receive through official channels instructions from your *mother*. Ah! ah! the Honorable Mayor! You're going to do things right, and for a start, every Sunday you're going to read your *Bulletins de la République* to all your National Guardsmen."[237]

Then she started dreaming about another paper. With Louis Viardot's help this time, she founded *La Cause du Peuple* with the collaboration of Victor Borie and Théophile Thoré, both staunch republicans.[238] "Our *home* is the public forum, or the press, in short, the soul of the proletariat,"[239] Sand repeated. The weekly paper began to appear on April 9, selling for twenty-five centimes, and it took a long time to set the type. There would be only three issues. In *La Vraie République* Sand also published a series of short articles stating her point of view on the events of the day, sometimes posing as a man or woman of humble origins. Very keen to report as closely as possible the opinions of the people she was defending, she urged them to make their demands known and to take part in political life. "Today," she wrote in the diary she was keeping at the time, "everything has really changed! [The workers] are involved in politics because politics today relates to work, to workers' lives."[240]

Again at the request of Étienne Arago, who, like the revolutionaries of 1789, saw theater as the ideal means of promoting ideas, Sand had a prologue entitled *The King Waits* [*Le roi attend*] performed at the Théâtre-Français, which had been renamed the

Théâtre de la République. While Louis XIV is kept waiting, which would have been most extraordinary, Molière is musing about monarchy and remarks: "What is a king? A man who has the power to do good, and only then does he stand out from other men."[241] After an imaginary dialogue with great playwrights of the past, Molière ends by saying that the genre of theater and the system of government both need to be changed. The first performance took place on 6 April, and it was free. The entire cabinet was in attendance; Pauline Viardot sang a *Marseillaise* of her own composition, and the actress Rachel performed the original national anthem. It was a great success. "The most beautiful thing about it was the audience, the workers scrubbed, calm, attentive, intelligent, sensitive, . . . more decent than the season-ticket holders of the Théâtre des Italiens or the Opéra,"[242] Sand observed, more delighted by the demonstration of this "fraternal republic"[243] that she had so earnestly desired than by her own success.

The *Bulletin de la République* that appeared on 15 April generated a burst of indignation because of the editorialist's radical opinions, and the political milieu knew just who she was. In this issue, number sixteen, Sand wrote that if the elections were too openly favorable to the bourgeoisie, their results should be tabled. It seemed hard for Sand not to try to stop conservative forces at any cost, even at the risk of jeopardizing the advent of democracy.[244] The opposition press flew into a rage, moderate republicans took exception, the caricatures and attacks aimed at Sand multiplied.[245] At Nohant a handful of conservatives threatened to break into her house and ransack it; Maurice, dismayed, reported this to his mother. In Paris the situation was becoming worrisome; people were seized with fear; the most insane rumors ran wild: "The National Guard is told that the suburbs are being pillaged; the suburbs hear that the communists are putting up barricades. True histrionics,"[246] Sand wrote to her son, who was having trouble getting his town council to accept his views: "Would there be much merit in making revolution if everything were to go swimmingly and we could have success without batting an eye?"[247] she asked.

On 28 April Sand went to City Hall [l'Hôtel de Ville], where she waited to hear the results of the elections that had taken place on the 23rd. She felt reassured by the calm reigning in the streets where political clubs had spontaneously sprung up. The news about the election delighted her: "All the members of the Provisional Government have been elected. Lamartine . . . , Ledru-Rollin . . . , Louis Blanc . . . , Perdiguier was elected in Paris and in Avignon. I hope that Gilland [one of the worker-poets] was elected in his department. Étienne Arago and Barbès have been elected in theirs. I am waiting impatiently for the results from Indre. . . . In short, the Republic will hold its own. But there'll be really quite a battle to wage, against the bourgeoisie."[248]

In truth, it was in particular moderate republicans who had won the day. On 4 May, Richard Monckton-Milnes, an English member of Parliament passing through Paris, organized a "literary luncheon"[249] in Sand's honor. Lamartine, Mérimée, and Alexis de Tocqueville were among the invited guests. A staunch liberal, Tocqueville gives in his *Recollections* [*Souvenirs*] an extremely interesting analysis of the period between the first signs of the February Revolution and the fall, in October 1849, of Odilon Barrot's ministry, of which he was himself a member. He left this description of the famous luncheon:

> Milnes put me beside Mme Sand; I had never talked to her; I even believe I had never seen her before (for I had not spent much time in the world of literary adventurers that she frequented). . . . I had great prejudices against Mme Sand, for I detest writing women, especially those who systematically disguise the weaknesses of their sex, instead of attracting our interest by showing themselves as they really are; despite this, I liked her. I thought her face looked rather heavy set, but her eyes were wonderful; . . . what especially struck me was finding in her something of the natural bearing of great minds. Indeed, her manners and language were truly simple, while she dressed with perhaps a bit of affected simplicity. . . . For a full hour we talked about public affairs, it being impossible to talk of anything else just then. Moreover, Mme

Sand was a sort of statesman; what she told me really made an impression; for the first time I was relating directly and familiarly with a person who could and would tell me something about what was going on in our adversaries' camp. . . . In great detail and with singular vivacity Mme Sand painted for me the state of the workers of Paris, their organization, number, and weapons, their preparations, thoughts, passions, and fearsome determination. I thought she was exaggerating, and she wasn't; what went on later proved that quite well.[250]

Even though Tocqueville did not hide his prejudices against women or his great mistrust of the "Montagnards," he nevertheless recognized that Sand really understood politics. Yet, as a woman, she had no legitimate basis for this. Having no right to vote, she could not aspire to any political office. A few determined women were dreaming of just that for an instant. In the paper that she ran, *La Voix des Femmes*, the Saint-Simonian Eugénie Niboyet urged Sand to run for the Chamber of Deputies with these words: "The representative around whom we rally is both man and woman: masculine in virility, feminine by God's intention, by poetry, we mean *Sand*. . . . She has made herself a man through strength of mind, she has remained a woman by being a mother. Sand is powerful and frightens no one; she's the one who must be called by the *wish of all women for the vote of all men*."[251]

Women lose their femininity and become like men if they use their minds, or else they are doomed to be double, *learned* on the one hand and *maternal* on the other. This is what the feminist Niboyet thought, and it remained one of the most stubborn prejudices, one shared by both men and women. One of Alcide Lorenz's caricatures in *Le Miroir Drolatique* sent the same basic message. There Sand is wearing a man's suit, although the trousers, vest, and frock coat emphasize her womanly shape; she holds a cigarette in one hand (using tobacco seems an obvious sign of transgression); a few titles of novels can be seen on the left; two posters bear the words "Chamber of Deputies" and "Chamber of Mothers." The caricature carries this ironical caption:

Si de George Sand ce portrait
Laisse l'esprit un peu perplexe,
C'est que le génie est abstrait,
Et comme on sait n'a pas de sexe.[252]

Sand's answer to Eugénie Niboyet's unexpected invitation appeared the same day in two newspapers directed by friends of hers, Louis Blanc's *La Réforme* and Théophile Thoré's *La Vraie République*. Her reply was brutal. Declaring that she did not know the ladies who were urging her to run, she hoped that "no elector would want to throw away his vote by yielding to the whim of writing [her] name on his ballot."[253] Yet the significance of the question had not escaped her. A few days later she addressed a long letter to the "members of the central committee" (the committee that nominated possible candidates on the left) in which she justified her refusal to aspire to any form of political power:

Must women one day participate in political life? Yes, one day, I think so . . . , but is that day close at hand? No, I don't think so, and for the condition of women to be so transformed, society must undergo a radical transformation. . . . For that to happen, won't women have to intervene politically from this day forward in public affairs?—I dare reply that this must not be, the reason being that social conditions are such that women could not honorably and loyally fulfill a political mandate. Women being the wards and dependents of their husbands through marriage, it is absolutely impossible for them to present guarantees of political independence. . . . So it strikes me as nonsense, begging the pardon of the persons of my sex who thought it necessary to proceed in this manner, to begin where one ought to finish, in order to finish apparently where one ought to have begun.[254]

Sand wanted women to participate in politics, but not before they had gained civil rights. Political rights made no sense to her until the most perfect equality ruled the relationship between men and women in private. At that time, as Sand well knew, women of Saint-Simonian inspiration were calling for civil and political rights for all women. They were also refusing marriage and displaying a certain freedom in matters of sexual conduct.

For her part, Sand categorically refused that "deplorable whim."[255] She defended marriage and the family, recalling her own experience only to denounce the slavery of the married woman who, physically and psychologically, did not belong to herself.[256] She made equality the sine qua non of all other rights and insisted: "The mother of a family, a minor at the age of twenty-four, finds herself in a ridiculous and humiliating position"; as for the rights of men over their wives, she qualified them as "savage, atrocious, antihuman."[257] In a letter to Hortense Allart, politically close to the Doctrinals and the author of an essay entitled *Women and Democracy in Our Time* [*La femme et la démocratie de nos temps*], Sand returned to this point: "As for me, I have but one passion, the idea of equality. . . . But it's a beautiful dream that I won't see realized. . . . Men aren't at that point. They are too resentful, too afraid, too petty."[258]

Yet Sand was undoubtedly "a sort of statesman" and found herself treated as such. An anonymous caricature depicted her dressed as a musketeer, in profile, with her eyes bulging; in her hair she wore the revolutionary cockade like an ornament, this being a little wink at the famous portrait that Auguste Charpentier had painted of her in 1838.

While she lunched with Alexis de Tocqueville, she also met with Alphonse de Lamartine several times. At the start she did not like the poet much and devoted a severe article to his *Poetic Meditations* [*Recueillements poétiques*] published in 1841.[259] When, in January 1843, Lamartine expressed open hostility toward the policies of Louis-Philippe's government and announced his plan to unify the Left, she hailed his determination and talents as an orator.[260] Upon closer view, she would still judge him too concerned with himself, too convinced of his own superiority. After 1848 the author would strike her as a "ridiculous old Narcissus,"[261] an "old schemer,"[262] and she would refuse all collaboration with him.

Behind a courteous facade the aristocrat from Burgundy was also quite wary of Mme Sand. Like Tocqueville, he was hostile to women who left the role that "nature" had assigned them. In his *Conversations About Literature* [*Cours familier de littérature*] Lamartine took to task the women who abandoned their children and forgot their saintly mission as mothers in order to go into politics. Sand, immoral and unnatural, had "lost her sex in the fray of genius,"[263] he wrote. The same old stubborn argument resurfaces.

The political climate was deteriorating day by day. On 15 May the radicals went for broke: the crowd marched into the Palais-Bourbon, and their leaders proclaimed the National Assembly dissolved. This aborted coup d'état led to a series of arrests. Barbès, Blanqui, and Raspail were put in prison. Forcefully disapproving the "deplorable madness" of her "friends in power,"[264] Sand feared with good reason that this would harden the positions of the conservatives and the moderate republicans. Dejected, maligned by those who saw a connection between her radical positions and the actions of her friends, she returned to Nohant two days later. For Sand, the revolution was finished, and, for the time being, so was her political activity. As she explained to Hortense Allart, "You are afraid of the republic as I would want it, and I am sadly resigning myself to the republic that you want if the people without enlightenment or enthusiasm decide to make a new lease with the past. Unlike you, I do not worship individual talent to the point . . . of taking proper names as beacons. . . . I appreciate your Guizot's talent, but I despise him; I read your Thiers with pleasure, but I don't trust him to make a success of my idea [equality]; and as for my idea, I have devoted my life to it, and I know quite well that it will be the death of me."[265]

Soon the specter of civil war gripped people's minds. Paris was unsettled; the provinces were worried. On 23 June the government decided to dissolve the National Workshops that guaranteed wages for men on public work-sites. In the following days the capital was shaken by violent street battles. A state of siege was declared, and the minister of internal affairs, General Cavaignac, decided to quash the insurrection. More than 5,000 died, thousands were arrested, and a certain number of insurgents were deported to Algeria. From then on the socialists were in the minority, while the liberals and the moderate republicans prevailed. As Sand wrote to Charles Poncy, "I was first so overwhelmed with disgust leaving Paris, then with horror learning the dreadful news about the June Days that I got sick and felt brain-dead for several days. I'm on my feet again, but my soul will be forever crushed, for I no longer have any hope for my remaining time on earth."

At the end of the year Louis-Napoléon Bonaparte was elected president of the Republic. "Let him frankly admit that he aspires to the throne, and France will see if she wants to reestablish the monarchy for the Bonaparte family,"[266] Sand had written a short time before in *La Réforme*, judging him to be an "enemy of the republican form of government by system and conviction."[267] The candidate trounced his rivals, Cavaignac, Ledru-Rollin, Raspail, and Lamartine. This fine victory astonished everybody, even those who were not in principle against him: "Republicans, legitimists, demagogues, gave him their votes," Tocqueville remembered, "for the nation was like a panic-stricken flock scattering aimlessly in all directions."[268]

As far as Sand was concerned, this election was proof that it was not yet time for an egalitarian and fraternal republic. Yet she was convinced that the people would not long tolerate a "reactionary" leader empowered solely by collective fear. Once again in *La Réforme* she made this comment on the event: "This enormous majority in favor of the one who among all the parties represents the Republic the least, what does this prove? At first sight, the answer must apparently be this: the majority of the French are not republicans; and this will no doubt be claimed by the party of the reaction. Well, they will be wrong . . . ; the proletarians are republican even so, and it won't be as easy as one thinks to take their sovereignty away from them."[269] There followed three difficult years of government during which freedom of expression was stifled and the opposition muzzled. To the great displeasure of Sand who was then in regular correspondence with Guiseppe Mazzini, one of the chief actors in the unification of Italy, France rushed to protect the Papal States from Garibaldi's army. General Oudinot's division reestablished papal sovereignty on 15 July 1849, an outcome that Sand judged "a thousand times sadder for France than for Italy."[270]

On 2 December 1851 Louis-Napoléon Bonaparte dissolved the National Assembly and invited the French people to confirm his move by plebiscite. Sand was then in Paris, attending the rehearsals of her play, *Victorine's Wedding* [*Le mariage de Victorine*], at the Théâtre du Gymnase. In the improvised diary that she kept for a few days, she analyzed the situation, observed what was going on in the streets, and noted: "I see the spirit of reaction like blind fate that has to be conquered through time and patience."[271] On 21 December, by an overwhelming majority, Bonaparte's deeds were confirmed. The Second Republic was dead. Disillusioned, Sand wrote to Pierre-Jules Hetzel: "After all, once the fundamental laws of a republic have been violated, a coup d'état, or to be more precise, a throw of the dice is no longer so illegitimate. With the end of universal suffrage, the right of assembly, and freedom of the press, we weren't really in a republic anymore, we were being governed by an oligarchy, and I don't like oligarchies anymore than empires."[272]

For a few months 1848 had realized the beautiful political ideal shared by Sand and her republican and socialist friends. The failure was particularly hard, and what followed only confirmed the fears of Sand, who, back at Nohant, kept a close eye on the nation and the strength of the Left. During this year a few family events also took place in the wings. Augustine Brault, the cousin whom Sand had come to see as her adoptive daughter, was married to André-Charles de Bertholdi. To help the young couple get settled, the "godmother" did not hesitate to go into debt. In February Solange delivered a little girl who lived only a few days, and the Clésinger couple ran into serious financial trouble and sold the hôtel de Narbonne that Solange had received as part of her dowry.

While Sand's son shared his mother's political convictions, her daughter did not. In the course of a long letter explaining her money problems, Solange slipped these words in, sure to get her mother's back up: "I don't view the men currently in power as disinterested beings, as citizens devoted body and soul to the good of the country. I see famous actors, clever players who forget the whole of the play they're performing in order to try to take center stage all alone. I confess, I don't feel much enthusiasm for this republic."[273]

In December 1848 Hippolyte Chatiron died of alcoholism, after having vegetated a while somewhere "between idiocy and madness."[274] Once Sand's rambunctious playmate, and later on more inclined to go out hunting or off to the cabaret with Casimir Dudevant than to remind him of his responsibilities as a husband, "the child of the little house" occupied a strange place in the life of his half sister. His name often showed up in her letters: most often Sand criticized his behavior and pitied his wife for having to put up with a desultory husband, sometimes violent, and excessively fond of drink. In Sand's letters to Hippolyte, she urged him to mend his ways, all the while assuring him of her unfailing support. During the unforgettable quarrel of July 1847 Hippolyte once again played an ugly part, intent on stirring up Solange's resentment against her mother. It is clear that he had become much more of a burden than an anchor for his half sister and the people around him. He spent his whole life in an awkward position, being a member of the Dupin family and at the same time an outsider, forever a bastard.

The next year one of Sand's plays was a great success at the Odéon Theater. The actors who loved putting on plays in Sand's parlor in Nohant inaugurated their new theater. After having talked to Prosper Mérimée, Sand managed to get Nohant-Vicq's little medieval church with all its frescoes on the national register of historic places. Chopin was dead, Solange gave birth to a second little girl named Jeanne-Gabrielle, and the birth of this child brought Sand and her daughter closer together.

In December 1849 two young men arrived in Nohant. The first was a German of commanding presence, a musician who was friends with Pauline Viardot and Hermann Müller-Strübing, of whom Sand seemed quite fond for a brief time. The second was the engraver Alexandre Manceau, one of Maurice's friends. Thirty-one years old, this man with delicate features, a balding head, and a jolly, conciliatory temperament, would spend the rest of his life with the mistress of the house. Her lover, secretary, as well as faithful and diligent factotum, he could organize theater performances at Nohant as handily as trips to Paris or family excursions. Painstakingly recording the activities of the famous woman he loved, he kept diaries from 1852 on, noting day after day and in great detail the slightest doings of the person he invariably referred to as "Madame." He would do this up to the time of his death.[275]

During the 1830s Sand had become a novelist and shown a lively interest in political and religious matters. She had separated from her husband and, while her two children were growing up, conducted her love affairs with great freedom. In the 1840s she stepped up the rhythm of her writing and raised her profile. The convictions that echoed through her novels were more markedly socialist, and her presence in the political arena more visible. Chopin's genius had reigned a moment over Nohant while Maurice was working in Delacroix's studio and when Solange married the sculptor Clésinger.

Sand left behind difficult years during which she, resolutely an *artist* in her tastes and demeanor, had led all kinds of battles, in politics, literature, and her personal life. In the early 1850s the political battles met defeat, for Sand and all those who shared her views. She still had her "love for work, family, and seclusion,"[276] Nohant, Maurice, Solange and her daughter, the friends who had always been there for her and in whose eyes she had nothing to be ashamed of, and, most of all, her immense talent as a storyteller. A thousand projects had taken shape and were now being realized, in novels and in plays, in which Sand was gradually coming to take an avid interest. Parlor theater and puppet theater occupied quite a place as well, mother and son working on them together. As for Alexandre Manceau, he was a thoughtful companion to a woman who knew what she was doing. It would be wrong to think that she was just subjugating a "child." The obvious discretion of Manceau, of whom Auguste Lehmann penciled a beautiful portrait, cannot be interpreted as lack of character. In truth, they were bit by bit building a solid, mutually fulfilling relationship. Love of their own accord, generously given and received, as Sand had always wished. On 7 July 1850 she wrote these words to Pierre-Jules Hetzel:

> Yes, I'm doing well, and I'm very happy, very happy. I really believe this is the first time in my life that I am conscious of the fact and can just let myself go a bit selfishly. . . . Up to now I had always been so devoted in my affections that I didn't even dream of asking myself if I was loving for my own pleasure. . . . I didn't go looking for what I've found; maybe I've deserved it because I've lived so unhappily and so patiently. . . . But, my heavens, it's so good to be loved and to be able to love totally. . . . I'm forty-six years old, I've got some gray hair, and that's no problem. Older women are loved more than the young ones, I now know this for a fact. It's not the person who has to last, it's love. God willing, this one will last, for it is good![277]

III

1852–1875

CONTINUITIES

Just after the coup d'état of 2 December 1851 there were thousands of arrests; attempts at insurrection in the nation's capital and the great provincial cities were nipped in the bud; and repression hit all levels of society—in particular, Edgar Quinet, Jules Michelet, and Adam Mickiewicz who were sacked from the Collège de France.

Sentenced to prison for their political activities, several of Sand's friends fled France. Pierre-Jules Hetzel took refuge in Brussels, where he remained until 1859, the year when amnesty was declared; Pierre Leroux went to England; Armand Barbès received a life sentence and went abroad as well; even though he was included in the amnesty, he would never return to France and died in Holland in 1870.[1]

Exiled by the decree of 9 January 1852 along with sixty-five opposition members of the Chamber of Deputies, Victor Hugo left Paris for Brussels and finally the Channel Islands. Enjoying greater visibility than anyone else, he would come to incarnate the opposition to the man he called "Napoléon le Petit" ["Napoleon the Small"]. As he warned in *Matters of Observation* [*Choses vues*], "M. Bonaparte should bear this in mind, he won't get the better of us. . . . We republicans and exiles, we are duty incarnate. M. Bonaparte had better come to terms with it; we've waged war against him from the rostrum, we've waged war against him in the streets, we'll wage war against him in the catacombs."[2]

Far removed from Hugo's circles, Sand, like Sainte-Beuve and Balzac, had scarcely expressed any admiration for the poet and playwright before this: "I read *Ruy Blas* [one of Hugo's plays] out of curiosity," she had written to Charlotte Marliani in 1839. "How stupid, absurd, insipid, and silly! More than ever pompous and trite!"[3] Hugo's strong resistance to Napoleon, whom he had at first supported, his subsequent exile, the publication of *History of a Crime* [*Histoire d'un crime*] and then *Napoleon the Small* [*Napoléon le Petit*] in 1852, kindled her interest and sympathy. At that point two of the period's great authors joined together in unconditional support of resisters and exiles, in defense of a democratic and republican form of government. "Men are evil . . . ," wrote Sand with regard to recent events. "The idea is good, and it will survive."[4]

A few letters exchanged every now and then after 1855 attest to the relationship between the two authors, brimming with respectful and polite formulas, especially on the part of Hugo, who really knew how to turn a compliment and couch his congratulations in verse.[5] Even so, Sand did not change her tune: "Lavish words touch me less than true feelings and clear ideas."[6] In 1863 she reviewed a book by Adèle Foucher-Hugo, *Victor Hugo According to a Witness of His Life* [*Victor Hugo raconté par un témoin de sa vie*]; the rather ambiguous article scarcely concealed her feelings about the poet.[7] "Hugo," she wrote later on, "thinks he has breathed new life into language; he has only found ways to express his own genius."[8] During the Second Empire, Sand and Hugo paid homage to each other for essentially political reasons. Sand sometimes appreciated Hugo's poetry, for instance, his *Contemplations*,[9] although she still considered him "too much the surgeon of his century."[10] Hugo sometimes defended Sand in the press and earned her sincere gratitude.[11] Joining together against their common enemies in less symbolic ways, such as paying each other a visit—even though Hugo invited Sand to come see him at Hauteville House[12]—that would never happen. Still there was respect, real respect, and neither one would try to conceal that fact. "Dear and great spirit, I love and venerate you,"[13] the author of *Les misérables* declared to Sand.

Sand managed to meet with Louis-Napoléon Bonaparte in order to make personal pleas for republican friends of hers who had been sentenced to death, life in prison, or deportation to Algeria. She also pleaded with him by letter, not hesitating to send the prince a "pained supplication"[14] in favor of those condemned to death or to appeal for leniency: "Order the release of all my compatriots from Indre. I have many friends among them, but let justice be done for every one."[15] She wrote again to Napoleon's nephew: "I am not Mme de Staël. . . . If you don't accept what people call my opinions (a terribly vague word for a mind's dreams or a conscience's meditations), I am at least certain that you won't come to regret believing that my heart is honest and unselfish."[16] She was occasionally given a hearing and received the support of the Count d'Orsay and Prince Jérôme, the cousin of the man who would soon be proclaimed emperor.

But more than ever Sand had to face harsh criticism from conservatives who could not pardon her interference in political matters, and from socialists as well. Her adversaries were delighted to add to the list of Mme Sand's scandals the mad resolve that had seized her at the start of a revolution fortunately nipped in the bud, nor were they about to forgive the infamous *Bulletin de la République*, where she called for putting the election results on hold if necessary. Printed in the thousands, the pamphlets of Adolphe Chenu (*Jérôme Paturot in Search of the Best of Republics* [*Jérôme Paturot à la recherche de la meilleure des républiques*]) and Louis Reybaud (*Les Montagnards de 1848*) had scathing words for Sand. The caricatures of Tony Johannot and Honoré Daumier in *Divorcing Women* [*Les divorceuses*] poked fun at her unseemly ambition. In *Les Contemporains*, a series devoted to celebrities of the time, Eugène de Mirecourt hailed Sand's talent in flattering terms, despite his disapproval of her politics: "Bear in mind, Madame," he wrote, "*progress* is a slow-growing fruit. You are wrong to join with those who stubbornly attempt to hasten its ripening in a hothouse."[17] Jules Barbey d'Aurevilly sneered later on in *The Bluestockings*: "If you believe what she says, she's nothing but a lovely dreamer, virginally pure of everything that she has been raked over the coals for. . . . She has genius, and she has innocence! Genius that we were so quick to buy! Innocence that we don't buy!

Now she has both. That's just as true, by God! as saying that she never wrote Ledru-Rollin's bulletins!"[18]

Without irony or insult, certain women took her to task for the same things. In France and elsewhere,[19] Sand served as a model who encouraged women to write. One of Alcide Lorentz's caricatures entitled "Woman of Letters at Work" ["Femme de lettres au travail"] bears this out. It shows an elegant young woman smoking a little clay pipe and holding a pen all the while contemplating an inkpot shaped like George Sand's head; twenty-some volumes bearing Sand's name are strewn across the floor. Her politics also met with mixed feelings. Alexandrine de Bawr, the author of several successful novels and plays, paid homage in *My Memories* [*Mes souvenirs*] to Sand's great narrative talents, nonetheless concluding: "Would to God that, instead of making every effort to wage bitter war on every social principle, Mme Sand had devoted her golden pen to the happiness of her fellow creatures! How proud she would have made us to be women, and what gratitude she would have earned from her contemporaries!"[20]

While she was appealing to the government for moderation, Sand ran into "lots of unpleasantness"[21] from the socialists and republicans who considered her dealings with Louis-Napoléon as betrayal. She wrote to Pierre-Jules Hetzel: "From far and wide everybody's writing to me: You are compromising yourself, you've gone astray, you're dishonoring yourself, you're for Bonaparte! *Appeal and win concessions for us*, but hate the man who grants them . . . , that inspires me with profound contempt and disgust for partisan behavior, and I most gladly offer . . . my *resignation from politics*."[22]

There were swarms of accusations and insults, and the press did not want to be left out. In September 1852 Sand asked Émile de Girardin if he would allow her to reply to all this in his newspaper *La Presse*:

I hope you don't think I get upset about literary criticism, but that you understand I have no wish to undergo more personal abuse. . . . It's fine with me if journalists bring whatever political hatred into their criticism of my ideas, that's what they have to do, but I don't want them saying that I'm impertinent, haughty, or crazy. . . . Every Monday these gentlemen have an open forum of invective for spewing their bile, and I don't know if I wouldn't be shown the door the day I might want to reply in one paper to the insults made in another one. Would it be indiscreet to ask if it would be a bother for you to let me stick my head out your window to say two words to the folks passing by? . . . Your paper is the only one I read, . . . the only one where I feel I could lodge a personal complaint.[23]

Her request was immediately granted.

Despite Sand's bitter remarks about these difficult times where "one half of France had denounced the other" and in which "Paris was total chaos, and the provinces a tomb,"[24] she still kept busy with literary projects of all kinds. Her fame had not diminished, she had more readers than before, and she would remain one of the great authors of the period for years to come. From a solely literary standpoint, 1848 probably looks more like a brief hiatus—for a few weeks Sand abandoned her many ongoing projects to deal with political matters exclusively and to act on some specific orders from the provisional government—rather than a real interruption. True, there is no doubt that her work bore the mark of a great hope, then profound disappointment, as we shall see. Yet it is important to note that everything that Sand would imagine and publish in the years after the revolution was already under way well before. Her writing reveals a steady rhythm of expansion and transformation, as two big book projects were about to show.

The first is the publication of the rustic novels. When Sand published *The Devil's Pool* in 1846—the very year that the Englishman William Thoms coined the term "folklore"—she had decided to set her "simple" stories in a Berrichon hamlet, thereby adapting the genre of *veillée* or after-supper tales traditionally associated with popular or children's literature. Momentarily dreaming of putting her four rustic novels together in a volume entitled *The Hemp-Beater's Tales*,[25] she had imagined a peasant narrator telling

things that he himself had seen. The preface to *La petite fadette* ends
with these words:

> The hemp-beater, having supped well, and seeing to his right a
> big pitcher of white wine, to his left a pot of tobacco so that he
> could fill his pipe whenever he felt like it that evening, told us
> the following story:
>
> Old Barbeau from La Cosse was doing pretty well, the proof
> being his seat on the town council. He had two fields that fed
> his family and turned a profit to boot. He cut enough hay in his
> meadows to fill cart after cart, and except for the grass along
> the edge of the stream choked by the rushes, it was considered
> first-rate fodder in these parts.
>
> Old Barbeau's house was well built with a tile roof. The air
> was wholesome up on the hill, and there was a garden with a
> good yield and a vineyard that would take a man six days to work.
> Down behind the barn he had . . .[26]

The love stories told by the hemp-beater are all quite similar.
The inventive plots all wind up with weddings, the protagonists
having overcome differences in rank and fortune to unite with their
beloveds. In *The Devil's Pool* a young servant marries a rich, widowed peasant; in *La petite fadette*, published in 1849 and dedicated
to Armand Barbès, a very poor girl who is a bit of a fairy (*fade* in
French) marries an identical twin from an affluent peasant family;
in *François the Waif* [*François le Champi*], published as a volume the
following year,[27] a "child abandoned in the fields"[28] marries the
rich peasant woman who took him into her home, a novel loved
by Marcel Proust as a child;[29] in *The Master Pipers*, published in
1853 and made up of thirty-two *veillées*, the humble Brulette, who
is first the girlfriend of Joset, a half-wit bagpiper, falls in love with
Huriel, a woodcutter's son, and becomes his wife at the end of
the tale. This last novel, the most elaborate of the rustic novels, is
Consuelo's counterpart as far as music is concerned, but this time
around Sand's enthusiastic descriptions are devoted to folk music,
with its inspired performers providing the impetus for the action.

The prefaces to *François the Waif* and *La petite fadette*, both written in the form of dialogues, ask two questions: How can one make a literary depiction of "rustic and natural life"?[30] What should one write now that the fine dream of an egalitarian society has faded? In the preface to *La petite fadette* Sand asserts, in the guise of a male writer: "After the dreadful June Days of 1848 I felt troubled and dismayed, down to the depths of my soul, by the storms outside and struggled to rediscover in solitude at least faith, if not tranquility. . . . I humbly confess that the certainty of a providential future cannot preserve an artist's soul from the pain of living through a here and now that civil war has darkened and torn asunder."[31]

In these hard times art acts like a balm, the poetry at its source being the only thing making it still possible to believe in an "ideal." A bit later, Sand writes: "Let's ever so gently celebrate such sweet poetry; let's press it out, like the sap of a salutary herb on humanity's wounds."[32]

The prefaces also advance two premises, already formulated several times over: Sand's interest in "primitive life" and the superiority of "primitive" art forms over all the others. "Certain Breton laments composed by beggars . . . prove that these simple souls had a more spontaneous and complete appreciation of truth and beauty than the souls of the most famous poets," she writes in the preface to *François the Waif*.[33]

This interest in "primitive art" and, more extensively, in every manifestation of Berrichon country life stems from an exceptional focus on a way of life she had known from childhood.[34] It also tallies with the curiosity shared by several artists of the period, such as Gérard de Nerval in his *Songs and Legends of the Valois* [*Chansons et légendes du Valois*], plus historians and the first ethnographers.

Berry played a significant role in the great wave of conserving, archiving, and collecting every form of folk art. This interest, shared by Sand and many others, got going in Brittany during Napoleon's Empire and kept on throughout the century. In 1842 Hippolyte-François Jaubert published his *Vocabulary of Berry* [*Vocabulaire du Berry*], followed in 1856 by his imposing *Glossary of Dialects in Central France* [*Glossaire des parlers du centre de la France*].

Sand, who later on drew up a lexicon of Berrichon expressions for her own use,[35] promptly congratulated him:

> For a long time I was thinking about doing a study of the gram-
> mar and syntax of our idiom, which I pride myself on knowing
> through and through, plus a dictionary. . . . I also believe that
> here [at Nohant] we speak pure Berrichon and the most primi-
> tive form of French. . . .
>
> I owe you the sincerest praise for rehabilitating and giving
> a new luster to our idiom, figures of speech, and some words,
> native inventions, whose subtlety eludes all translation. Fafiot,
> fafioter, berdin (I think it should be written *bredin* because we
> say *beurdin*, like *peurnez*, prenez, *bourdouiller*, bredouiller, *deurser*,
> dresser), give very fine nuances of irony, and I challenge the
> whole French Academy to find us the equivalent.[36]

In 1845 *L'Éclaireur de l'Indre* published Laisnel de La Salle's *Legends and Beliefs of Central France* [*Légendes et croyances du centre de la France*]. Between 1851 and 1855 Sand published in *L'Illustration* five articles on customs in Berry (especially with regard to wed-dings, already described in *The Devil's Pool*), but also on the specific character of the region and its inhabitants.[37] "I was honored or rather gratified to hear sometimes . . . that I had been Berry's Walter Scott,"[38] she recalled, alluding to the great writer's role in promoting the culture of Scotland.

Sand applauded when in 1852 the minister of public instruc-tion decided to collect folk songs. In the past she had invited Chopin and Pauline Viardot to do the same during a visit to Nohant, and she herself had noted on music paper the tunes of some Berrichon songs. She wrote, once again, in *L'Illustration*: "In our opinion it would be absolutely necessary to publish the musical score. In folk songs the words are so airy that they have no appeal when read, but if you hear them sung, they surprise, charm, or thrill you."[39]

Still, as the true creator she was, Sand remembered, observed, and transformed. Characterized as rustic and primitive, the hemp-beater's language is a remarkable work of style. Sand not only incorporated Berrichon expressions—there are about a hundred in *La petite fadette*: *accoté, affener, agasse, amiteux, aumaille, bavousette, bouchure, brebiage*, etc.—but also words found in Rabelais and Montaigne, a few deliberate solecisms, and some pure and simple lexical inventions. The syntax is spare, intentionally archaic, and the characters' speech is sown with plant and animal metaphors. Deeply committed to verisimilitude, the portrait of Berry also displays some metamorphosis through literary creation. "There is no more truth," Sand declared, "in reality made ugly than in a prettified ideal."[40]

That sentence is a good summary of her aesthetics and the ideas she put forward in her letters to Champfleury, who published *Miss Mariette's Adventures* [*Les aventures de Mlle Mariette*] in 1854. A fervent defender of Gustave Courbet, Champfleury was one of the first to make realism into "a war machine" for driving a great modern revolution in the arts. It is worth taking the trouble to understand Sand's arguments. They demonstrate that her choices were perfectly conscious. A realist when describing the peasant world and an idealist when illustrating her political convictions in the novel, she was also convinced by the need for beauty: art transfigures reality, Sand repeated, and there's no need to make it ignoble. No doubt such an aesthetic program means that she belonged to the Romantics, from whom the "realists" endeavored to set themselves apart. Yet, more fundamentally, it stems from a deep conviction, even an existential need. Sand, in *Story of My Life*, formulated it in these terms:

> Poetry is the condition of my existence, and everything that too cruelly kills the dream of things good, simple, and true, which alone sustain me against the horror of this century, is a torture that I try to dodge as much as possible.
>
> Whenever I've had the freedom to choose how to be, I've endeavored to idealize the reality around me and to make it a sort of fictive oasis where evil people and idlers would not be tempted to enter or to stay. A Golden Age dream, a mirage of

rustic innocence, in art or poetry, has had me in its grip from
earliest childhood and followed me into adulthood.[41]

In October 1858, under the title *Country Legends* [*Légendes
rustiques*], Sand published another twelve Berrichon legends with
resonant names such as *The Foolish Stones* [*Les pierres-sottes*], *The
Women Who Wash by Night* [*Les laveuses de nuit*], *The Leader of
Wolves* [*Le meneu' de loups*], *The Monk of Étang-Brisses* [*Le moine
des Étangs-Brisses*], and *Hobgoblins* [*Les flambettes*].[42] She felt it was
urgent to write them down before they were totally forgotten. As
she wrote to Maurice, "These things get lost as peasants become
enlightened, and it is good to save a few versions of this great poem
of the supernatural from oblivion, fast upon us. Humanity fed on
the supernatural for such a long time, and while country folks don't
know it, they are its last bards nowadays."[43]

Maurice, nicknamed "Bouli," who "want[ed] only to be a
painter,"[44] had shared his mother's interest in Berrichon folklore
for a long time. Since childhood he had been drawing pictures of
Berry (and visitors to Nohant), and he went on capturing with the
stroke of a pencil everything that struck his eye. With Sand's enthusiastic recommendations, he gradually earned a reputation as an
illustrator. The Berrichon countryside, peasants at work, oxen with
all their trimmings, seasonal occupations, the music of bagpipes
and hurdy-gurdies, the bourrée and other traditional dances, the
cabbage festival, the fairgrounds, as well as the legends still being
recounted became the subject of lots of drawings, many of which
appeared in the press.

Maurice, who had studied with Delacroix, also made oil paintings of the same subjects. At the Salon of May 1853 and again in
1857 he exhibited *Berrichon Mule-drivers* [*Muletiers berrichons*].[45]
Even though he was not uncommonly talented, Maurice shared
the interests of his time. His productions were contemporary
with Millet's *The Winnower* [*Le vanneur*], *Sheaf-Makers* [*Botteleurs*],
and *Women Gleaning* [*Glaneuses*]. (The resemblance between
Sand's "filthy peasants" and the Barbizon painter's "innocent convicts" did not escape Huysmans, who considered them equally

"contrived."[46]) Maurice provided the artwork for his mother's articles in *L'Illustration* as well as her *Country Legends*. The original wash drawings are hanging in the dining room at Nohant.

Story of My Life is the second undertaking that kept Sand busy before and after the revolution. On the advice of Pierre-Jules Hetzel, she began writing her autobiography in April 1847. In December of the same year she confided to Charles Poncy: "I've taken on a long-term project entitled *Histoire de ma vie*. It's a series of things remembered, professions of faith, and meditations. It will all be framed with fairly poetic and very simple details."[47]

This was an extraordinary gesture. Aside from a few memoirs published by female aristocrats during the Restoration—for example, Félicité de Genlis's *Unpublished Memoirs on the Eighteenth Century and the French Revolution* [*Mémoires inédits sur le dix-huitième siècle et la Révolution française*] in 1825—women had never launched into some great "story of myself" like Rousseau in his *Confessions*, Chateaubriand in his *Memoirs from Beyond the Tomb* [*Mémoires d'outre-tombe*] or Dumas in his *Mémoires*. (Stendhal's unfinished autobiography, *The Life of Henri Brulard* [*Vie de Henri Brulard*], would not be known until the end of the century.)

Her work had scarcely begun when Pierre-Jules Hetzel started seeking a publisher for this ambitious project. Initially thought to be as long as Lamartine's eight-volume *History of the Girondins* [*Histoire des Girondins*], it would turn into a complicated production.[48] While Sand was exchanging letters with René de Villeneuve to learn more about her family, the Revolution of February 1848 burst upon the scene. She dropped the project, starting it back up again on 1 June 1848, a few days after her return to Nohant. Chapter 8 of the second part is not silent on these recent events:

> If I had finished this book before the Revolution, I dare say it would have been something different, the book of a loner, a generous child, for I had only known humankind through the study of often exceptional individuals and whom I had always examined at leisure. Since the Revolution my eyes have campaigned through the world of facts, and that has made me another person.

... So my book will be gloomy if I stick with my recent impressions. But who knows? time quickly marches on, and, when all is said and done, people are no different from me, meaning they get discouraged and cheer up again with great facility.[49]

In 1854 Émile de Girardin finally acquired the rights to *Story of My Life* for his newspaper. Chateaubriand's *Memoirs from Beyond the Tomb* had appeared in the same venue, at rather irregular intervals, between October 1848 and February 1850, followed by the *Memoirs* of Dumas starting in the summer of 1852, both of them devoting a few pages to Sand.[50] *Story of My Life* started running in *La Presse* on 5 October 1854. In total, it was published in 138 installments, up through June 1855, and was such a huge success that people would rip the newspaper out of each other's hands. A caricature of five men in top hats trying to read an issue held by a cap-wearing worker came out in *Le Journal pour Rire*, with the caption: "Great success for George Sand's *Story of My Life*. A few enthusiastic and impatient fans even made a deal to see the printer's proofs so they'd be the first to know." At the end of October 1854 the Lecou publishing house started publishing the work in paperback as well. The complete first edition was twenty volumes long.[51]

When Sand began writing her autobiography, she told her friend Charlotte Marliani: "This is a history of my life (not CONFESSIONS). . . . It's quite enough to tell my inner life (*as an artist*) and as an intellectual, without turning the public into my intimate confidant. My book will be serious and useful."[52] *Story of My Life* does not contradict this declaration. From the start Sand stresses the interest of *each and every* life and turns autobiography into a democratic activity, far from the haughty memoirs of aristocrats in the past: "You artisans who are beginning to understand everything, you peasants who are starting to learn how to write, don't forget your dead ancestors any longer. Pass the lives of your fathers on to your children . . . ! The trowel and the billhook are emblems as beautiful as the horn, the tower, or the bell. . . . Write your stories, all you who have understood your life and searched your heart."[53]

Next she underscores the privileged place that "the inner life, the life of the soul, meaning the story of one's own heart and spirit, . . . the personal impressions, the voyages or attempted voyages in the abstract world of mind and feeling," will have in her autobiography.[54] Finally, even if she devotes a few pages in the last chapter of *Story of My Life* to Chopin's character, she doesn't mean to provide any kind of detail about her private life: "Vis-à-vis the public, I have no right to the past experience of all the people whose lives have been linked with mine,"[55] this she definitely wants to make clear. So she evokes her conflicts with Casimir Dudevant in a few lines and does the same for the event that attracted the most media attention, her affair with Alfred de Musset.

Her curious family history, her grandmother, her tutor Deschartres and the impetuous Sophie, her maid and her half brother Hippolyte, her games with the peasant children of Nohant, her pranks at the convent of English Sisters along with Mary G***, came flooding back in lively fashion. Later on, her grandmother's death, her wedding, the birth of her two children, her literary débuts, the personalities of Marie Dorval, Michel de Bourges, Balzac, Delacroix, and many others that she met in the course of her career, became the subject of particularly incisive portraits. No doubt, swept along by the indomitable will to be "a woman who writes,"[56] Sand knew how to tell great stories, but she also knew, with rare acuity, how to analyze her hopes and fears, to express the pain that the long enmity between her mother and grandmother caused her, as well as the depression into which she fell, despite "Corambé's" intervention, between the end of her adolescence and the first years of her literary life. "Nobody has gone further than you in these analyses," Gustave Flaubert would write to her later on. "*Story of My Life* has tremendously profound pages on that score."[57]

During the years between the end of the July Monarchy and the beginning of the Second Empire Sand took considerable interest in the distribution of her works and the means of making them available to all. Political and financial considerations underlay several ambitious publishing projects with Pierre-Jules Hetzel, a key figure for understanding her choices about books and editions.

Having become a sort of literary agent for Sand before the Revolution of 1848, he was a sure and faithful friend, often her confidant for personal problems. Keeping a close eye on how the book market functioned, very creative in matters of publishing (having started as a publisher in 1843, he continued working in Brussels after the coup d'état), he helped Sand negotiate her contracts with directors of newspapers and journals and watched over her finances, specifically the income she could earn from her publications, and the strict observance of contractual agreements, with the help of the lawyer Gabriel Falampin on this point.

Two publishing projects took shape through the years: the first being the broad distribution of certain of Sand's works in an inexpensive format ("This will let us popularize works written in good part for the working classes, but read only by the bourgeoisie, thanks to the publishers' stupid and aristocratic speculations"[58]); the second being the sale of her literary capital to a publisher who would take charge of its use, freeing Sand from repeated negotiations with various directors of serials or reviews, then various publishers ("That would deliver me from the details of business, and I'd invest my money"[59]).

The first project came to a successful conclusion in September 1851 when three publishers, Blanchard, Hetzel, and Marescq, agreed, despite various problems, to publish her *Illustrated Works* [*Œuvres illustrées*].[60] Printed on large sheets of paper with two columns in small fonts, each volume cost twenty centimes, like the recently created "penny dreadfuls." For each novel Sand composed a new preface or note. Hetzel decided to entrust the illustrations, all wood engravings, to Tony Johannot, much appreciated in the profession. Despite that, Sand managed to get "Mauricot"[61] hired as Johannot's associate and then, after the latter's death in 1852, as the sole illustrator, notwithstanding the publisher's and engravers' clear reservations about Maurice's designs, whose faint strokes would be difficult to reproduce. Nine volumes, each one containing several novels and short stories, would appear between 1851 and 1856. Along with those of Balzac, Hugo, and Sue, Sand's volumes had the biggest print runs, 20,000 copies on average.[62]

In just fifteen years, thanks to a series of technical innovations and fierce competition between the publishers Gervais Charpentier, Michel Lévy, and Louis Hachette, the price of books had gone down considerably. Meanwhile, readership was increasing and becoming markedly more diversified. Determined to take advantage of this little revolution in publishing, Sand resolutely stepped into "industrial" literature so reviled in certain sectors. Above and beyond the project of her *Illustrated Works*, she signed contracts with the publisher Lecou to make her work available in the so-called Charpentier format, the ancestor of paperbacks, without any illustrations this time, as well as with Louis Hachette for the sale of certain titles in the brand-new "Railroad Library" ["Bibliothèque des chemins de fer"], another way to assure the broad distribution of her novels.

At the beginning of the 1850s Sand was also trying to trade on and protect the capital that her work represented, for she was afraid that after her death Maurice and Solange, who did not get along, might liquidate her estate and wind up damaging their positions in such an operation.[63] The letters to Émile Aucante, Sand's intermediary with Parisian publishers, demonstrate endless strategies for ensuring both her liberty as an author and the market value of her existing body of work, "manuscripts, . . . novels, plays, in short, *everything*."[64] Walter Scott had lost everything after his publisher went bankrupt, and Sand did not intend to suffer the same fate and to be forced "to work herself into a stupor."[65] In 1855, after several attempts to deal with "the huge question of literary property,"[66] Michel Lévy, then the biggest mainstream publisher in Paris, proposed publishing Sand's work in two inexpensive series. Five years later, a contract made him Sand's designated editor for the rest of her career.

Keeping up with developments in newspaper and book publishing and determined to keep her place there, Sand was a remarkable businesswoman. Hoping to make good use of the money she had worked hard to earn, she also acted as the head of her household, eager to bequeath to her children what she had acquired as a writer.

THE PERFORMING ARTS

On the occasion of the first performance of the *Devil in the Family* [*Démon du foyer*] Sand wrote to Émile de Girardin: "At the age of forty-eight I'm starting a new *career*: theater. People don't want me to have a place there, but I want it, and I'm going to have it."[67]

This remark has to be read in a context of controversy and failure. The coup d'état of December 1851 had interrupted the performances of *Victorine's Wedding* at the Théâtre du Gymnase. In March 1852 Sand's comedy, *Pandolphe's Vacation* [*Les vacances de Pandolphe*] had next to no success with the public, even though it was inventive and funny. Then Sand tried an "Italian comedy in a Watteau setting,"[68] and it too was a failure. The critics obviously had a hard time reconciling Sand's politics during the Revolution of 1848 with comedies of the sort that owed a lot to Molière, Marivaux (the plays involving servants and peasants), and Sedaine.[69]

Theater was then considered one of the most popular forms of entertainment, exciting dreams of money and success for others besides well-known playwrights. From Stendhal to Zola, nearly all the men of letters wanted to write for the stage. Few women of the time, except for Sand, Virginie Ancelot, Delphine de Girardin, Mélanie Waldor, and Alexandrine de Bawr, wrote plays, and that was because of the way that plays were produced. There was nothing simple about the theater world. It was hard to attract and keep an audience. The audiences, by turns severe or good-natured, attentive or indifferent, had grown considerably more diverse, and there were more and more theaters in Paris. Musset's *Night in Venice* [*La nuit vénitienne*] and Hugo's *The Burgraves* [*Les Burgraves*] had been failures; Flaubert's *The Candidate* [*Le candidat*] flopped, and so did Zola's adaptation of *Thérèse Raquin*.

Sand made her first foray into theater in April 1840 when *Cosima or Hatred in Love* [*Cosima ou la haine dans l'amour*], a five-act drama, opened at the Théâtre-Français with Marie Dorval in the starring role. It had a short run, only seven performances. Sand, who had already written several novels "in dialogue form," claimed at the time that she had been "made to go where she didn't want

to go,"[70] in other words, that she had been persuaded to put on a
play that was not really meant for the stage.

Nine years later she tried again. This time she wrote an adaptation of *François the Waif* for the stage, and it was performed at
the Théâtre de l'Odéon and directed by Pierre Bocage. "A witty
little thing," that's what Sand called her "pastoral in three acts,"[71]
with the beginning of the plot rewritten. She also brightened it up
with some "little Berrichon melodies,"[72] much to the audience's
liking, that she had personally transcribed. Her friend François
Rollinat, who attended the play on 24 November 1849, wrote
to her: "*Champi* is a huge success: the audience was moved, they
laughed and they cried. . . . It's not so much socialist talk that
makes it a complete success, but . . . the play's charm and matchless
simplicity."[73] Sand's comic plays owe a lot to the *commedia dell'arte*
and its avatars in the Théâtre-Italien. There she found what she
especially liked, "a study of real character types,"[74] as she explained
in the preface to Maurice's book, *Masks and Clowns* [*Masques et
bouffons*], with its fine illustrations. With this she mixed in classi-
cal references, most obviously Molière, whom she always greatly
admired—he had the main role in *The King Awaits* [*Le roi attend*]
and was the subject of a play performed at the Théâtre de la Gaîté
in May 1851.[75] Sand's dramas, on the other hand, were inspired
by "bourgeois" drama from the end of the eighteenth century and
Romantic melodrama. In any case, all her plays displayed her political convictions, especially with regard to the condition of women.
Sometimes the concoction looks rather curious.

Sand's theater was not just a question of genre, but also of
geography. Sand's plays were set in Berry or often Italy. *The
Devil in the Family*, for instance, takes place in "a little villa near
Milan."[76] *Villageoiserie* or "village thingamabob," that's what Sand
called a "dramatic and comic"[77] play like *François the Waif* that made
the audience laugh and cry and brought to the Paris stage the
way people lived and talked in Nohant and nearby hamlets. So
too *Claudie*, which opened in January 1851 at the Théâtre de la
Porte-Saint-Martin, with Bocage playing the role of Old Rémy,
an eighty-year-old man bringing in the harvest, and *The Winepress*

[*Le pressoir*], which opened in September 1853 at the Théâtre du Gymnase.[78] *Claudie* was a resounding success and would be performed again in 1926 at the Comédie-Française, while the second, praised by the critics, was not greatly appreciated by the public. In any case, Sand wanted her plays to educate the audience, the often edifying moral leaving no doubt about the author's intentions.

Sand probably did not have a true theory of theater, as Diderot and Hugo did.[79] Yet her ideas about theater are often expressed in the prefaces to her published plays, in the general preface to the three-volume set of plays published by Lévy in 1866, her correspondence, and numerous passages from her novels, especially when they are about theater. In 1851 *The Castle in the Wilderness* [*Le château des désertes*] puts a troupe of amateur actors on stage, and Sand acknowledged that she wanted "to stir up some ideas about theater."[80] There are more similarities than differences between theater and novels, as is shown by the way they echo each other. Then again most of Sand's plays were adapted from her novels, with a simplified plot and dialogues revised for the stage.

Going from the manuscript to opening night was no small affair, as Sand soon found out. The ink would be scarcely dry when she had to connect with a theater director and try and interest him in her play. Next, the two of them had to go over the contract point by point and come to agreement about the author's royalties, the length of the run, the conditions relating to the noncompetition clause. Finally, the opening date had to be scheduled after taking into account the programming calendar and the actors' availability. After all that, the rehearsals could start, at the Théâtre du Gymnase directed by Adolphe Lemoine-Montigny, or the Théâtre de la Gaîté, the Vaudeville, the Théâtre de la Porte-Saint-Martin, or the Odéon.[81] As Sand observed, "People . . . generally believe that every movement and intonation is freely improvised at the time of performance. They don't know that the long and painstaking work of rehearsals aims to imprison the actor, to tie him down to the conventions of his role with automatic precision."[82]

When rehearsals began, Sand usually left Nohant for Paris—as discreetly as possible.[83] Leaving nothing to chance, she would make her views clear on the staging, decor, lighting, costumes, and props. On this last point, she would give precise details by letter, along with designs, sometimes with Maurice's help. On 15 November 1849, a few days before the opening of *François the Waif*, she wrote to Bocage:

> Dear friend, I'm sending you the bonnets and necessary instructions, for your ladies. The chair is shown in the design, *Madeleine's costume*, that Maurice sent you. It's a wooden armchair with leather or straw trimmings and little canvas cushions. In Berry there is nothing particular or special about these old pieces of furniture. . . . The footstool is part of the armchair and rolls along with it. . . .
>
> *General remarks about women's bonnets.*
>
> All the bonnets have to be held up by a stitched underpiece, just like the one I'm sending you. Between the underpiece and bonnet there's got to be a headband of the same size and shape in white or black silk for mourning, in pink or pale blue satin for dressy occasions. . . . Don't take the done-up bonnet apart without paying close attention to how it was put together. Everything is in the way the chinstraps are tied. . . . Mariette shouldn't have any lace in the first act, but there is no need to have her chinstraps tied back, that's especially for widows.[84]

While true-to-life costumes were important for Sand, she also kept a watchful eye on the music, especially the Berrichon melodies for the rustic plays. She even composed the final rondeau for *Pandolphe's Vacation*.[85] Anxious to be true to the region down to the slightest details, she took great pains with the little particulars that give an impression of authenticity. In so doing, she created "regionalist" theater, and if today it strikes us as quaint, that is no doubt because of her political resolve to show the lower classes, villagers or peasants, as fundamentally good and generous.

She knew a good number of actors and kept a close eye on casting. In her opinion, Frédéric Lemaître, Pierre Bocage, and Bouffé were among the best, along with Rachel, Rose Chéri, and Sylviane

Arnould-Plessy.[86] She also liked the Bertons, father and son, and kept in touch with the children of Marie Dorval who were also on the stage. *The Winepress* was written, she wrote, "for Geoffroy, Lesueur, Lafontaine, Bressant, and Dupuis, . . . I see them in these roles."[87] *Master Favilla* [*Maître Favilla*], performed at the Odéon in 1855, was dedicated to the actor Antoine Rouvière, who had the starring role.

As Sand knew, an actor is a physique and a voice—tone, diction, and sometimes an accent—a particular way of moving on stage, gesturing, and expressing emotion; it is also a form of "intelligence" that can, as in the case of Marie Dorval, have "amazing psychological depth with subtle and profound observations."[88] True "*art*" is not the same thing as "*artifice*,"[89] she insisted. The most important thing is to play it *right* and therefore stay "in character."[90]

On opening night Sand always held her breath: "A performance will always be a roll of the dice . . . if your artistic conscience is without reproach, you can stay very calm and take bad luck with tons of philosophy."[91] Applauded or booed, the play would run for days, weeks, or months, during which Sand would be pleased or put out by its critiques. Sometimes she would rethink certain lines and draw up a list of changes for the theater director: "This would only take you and your fine actors fifteen minutes,"[92] she noted in a letter to Bocage about *François the Waif.*

Once she had become a playwright, Sand still enjoyed going to the theater. In years past she had admired Marie Dorval in her few great roles in Romantic plays; she even applauded Pauline Viardot in numerous operas. She gladly attended the plays of her friends—Alexandre Dumas fils, Paul Meurice, and Auguste Vacquerie, with all of whom she had a correspondence—but also many other resounding or minor successes of the time. Yet she did not owe her excellent knowledge of all the theater trades just to the actors she knew and her powers of observation. It was also the product of her long-standing practice of parlor theater starting at Nohant in December 1846.

In the beginning it was just family entertainment, various pantomimes with musical accompaniment. As Sand explained to Emmanuel Arago,

Every evening I have a ballet to compose. We put on the right costumes; I am the orchestra leading the pantomime on the piano, with various tunes *ad libitum* such as *Malbrough s'en va-t-en-guerre*, *J'ai du bon tabac*, *Au clair de la lune*, etc., etc. The actors are Maurice, Lambert, Titine [Augustine Brault], and Fernand [de Preaulx, Solange's fiancé]. Solange, not wanting to budge, is the audience; I'm the orchestra, the poet, the prompter, the director, the stage manager, etc. . . . Every evening we put on a new play. I write it over dessert; we learn our parts over coffee. We get our costumes on at ten, which is the most time-consuming and the most fun; the play is performed at midnight; then we have a late supper and go to bed at two.[93]

Even though this kind of entertainment was the delight of eighteenth-century châteaux, the one-woman orchestra's powers of invention were still remarkable, like her love of disguise and role-playing that this activity naturally invited. Playing at being someone else by momentarily donning the appropriate costume, in addition to doing everything else simultaneously—here, all the trades and crafts associated with the stage and then exercised exclusively by men—all this obviously stems from a powerful injunction that resonates throughout the whole of Sand's life.

The theater at Nohant started rather informally: at first they entertained themselves in the evening with mimes, especially Chopin's; then came the more or less improvised playlets and pantomimes with musical accompaniment—Maurice and his friend Eugène Lambert,[94] whom Sand met in Delacroix's studio and who soon became like an adoptive son to her, were glad to get involved. Next came the sketches, with greater demands for the amateur actors and more ambitious plans from the stage manager. In 1850 Sand redesigned the ground floor of the château at Nohant, knocking down the wall between Casimir's old bedroom and the storage room and setting up a real stage with wings, scenery, and a curtain, plus enough space for several rows of seats out in front. A loft, accessible by a little wooden staircase, served as a dressing room for the actors.

A real miniature theater, the Nohant playhouse seemed like the ideal place for trying out a scene or a line, testing a comic or poignant situation, gauging the challenges of a certain role. It became a laboratory for the plays that would be performed in Paris. As Sand explained to Solange,

> Sometimes I say to hell with my plays because out of every two weeks they take up two or three days that I'd prefer to devote to work. . . . But . . . I've found our theater useful, and it's given me rather good notions, maybe not about scene arrangement, but about situations the audience may find especially interesting or funny. That's what I think, in any case, and I believe our improvisation method is a fine way of preparing. I let Maurice do nearly all the plays, just giving him a hand when he gets himself in a real mess. . . . A scene tucked in the right place and with the right words has a charming effect, and the actors are all amazed that it seems so effortless. You just can't imagine the progress we've made here and how things are now coming together so well.[95]

Most of Sand's plays that were performed in theaters in the 1850s were first staged at Nohant. Aside from Sand, the troupe was Manceau, Maurice, and Lambert, plus some old friends and houseguests, Charles Duvernet, Victor Borie, and the painter Léon Villevieille. The household help was glad to get involved, for example, Marie Caillaud. Like Sand, they all enjoyed putting on costumes, wigs, and makeup. Maurice made a pen drawing of actors dated January 1850 in which twenty-odd people are gathered around a table. Sand is at the center of the group, with Manceau standing to her left. The caption reads: "From the start Manceau poses as the director of the Nohant troupe. The rules are read, to which many loud complaints are heard."[96]

The amateurs sometimes got help from seasoned actors, like Pierre Bocage or somebody else from Paris. This was the case when *Victorine's Wedding*, imagined as a sequel to Sedaine's *The Philosopher in Spite of Himself* [*Le philosophe malgré lui*] was being written. Lacking someone to "play a nice short little part,"[97] Sand wrote to Pierre-Jules Hetzel: "Find us a little student from the Conservatory, not ugly, nice, unassuming, good-natured, who'll come give us a hand or earn a few pennies, as he wishes, and who in any case will just like coming along for the ride. . . . You know how we put on our plays, in a very homey way that doesn't require actors, rather a kind of calm on-stage group reading. . . . You come along too if you're free; we want to put the play on from the 15th to the 20th of this month [September]. All the costumes, wigs, rouge, etc. that he may need are here."[98]

Even though he wasn't the head of the troupe, Maurice was nevertheless the kingpin of Nohant's parlor theater. With help from Eugène Lambert, he built traditional decors painted in tempera. Plus, he assisted his mother in each stage of a new play's production, from writing the sketch up through the first performance. He also elaborated lots of original costumes with her, as one can see in two albums of his watercolors at the Bibliothèque nationale de France.

The theater was not just a laboratory for the plays performed in Paris. It had its own repertory as well. Most of the manuscripts we now possess were written by Sand,[99] but Maurice occasionally corrected or modified his mother's scenarios. As Sand explained, "Often I do nothing more than arrange the order of the scenes that they [the actors of the troupe] ask me to play and help make their own ideas feasible. It's a genre where the *author* completely disappears, theater where *everybody* is an author."[100]

Fewer in number, Maurice's sketches put to use the most traditional dramatic devices; Sand occasionally intervened in order to fix a monologue or to suggest some stage directions. Maurice loved stories about bandits, fantastic dramas, rustic comedies directly inspired by life at Nohant, comic scenes in a make-believe setting in Italy or the Orient. Maurice's sole purpose was to have a good time and to give the audience a good laugh.

People familiar with Nohant, "guests" and denizens of the village, made up a heterogeneous audience that sometimes reached fifty or more. They received an invitation with the heading "Theater of Nohant" and the title of the play to be performed as well as a seat number. Maurice was responsible for the little theater bills calligraphed on blue or grayish-brown paper. One of them read:

Nohant Mlle Ida's Return to the Stage 5 October 1856
DON'T PLAY WITH FIRE!!
[IL NE FAUT PAS JOUER AVEC LE FEU!!]
drama in two scenes[101]

In 1865 Sand wrote a preface for an edition of five plays entitled *Theater of Nohant* [*Théâtre de Nohant*]. The first play, *The Hobgoblin* [*Le drac*], a charming fantasy about a phantom, was dedicated to Alexandre Dumas fils. She wrote: "You came and loved that way of telling a dream and acting it out for a family reunion, a little bit like telling stories about yourself in front of the fire. So I dare publish this play, and putting it under the protection of your indulgence, I dedicate it to you, . . . as to a fine friend whose sense of aesthetics accepts and understands all artistic license without being the least pedantic."[102]

A true collective undertaking, the theater of Nohant was less improvisation than a sort of experimental theater whose entertainment value must not be underestimated, for example, *Plutus*, dedicated to Alexandre Manceau and starting off with a wacky dialogue between Aristophanes and Mercury. They of course tried out plots and lines for the stage in Paris, but they all had fun, loads of it, with fantasy plays imitating various subjects and mimicking the way real theater was performed. It was obviously a *game*, but a complex game in which certain actors were not amateurs, where Sand, as the stage manager, often on stage as one can see in Maurice's watercolors, was not just writing for fun, where the people close to her, all of them "artists" in some sense or other, showed remarkable invention in making scenery, costumes, and parodies of what goes on in the theater.

There was another sort of theater that Maurice started concocting at the close of 1847. As Sand recalled in *The Puppet Theater of Nohant* [*Le Théâtre de marionnettes de Nohant*], "For the first time, with help from Eugène Lambert, and no audience aside from

Victor Borie and me, Maurice set up a puppet stage in our old parlor. . . . There were just the four of us at home: two of us devoting ourselves to making the long winter evenings an enchantment for the two others."[103]

Maurice's first little puppet stage was "a chair with its back to the audience and the two kneeling puppeteers hidden behind a huge drawing portfolio and a towel"; and the puppets were nothing more than "two sticks smoothed down just a bit and wrapped in rags."[104] Yet, because of the success of the hilarious, inventive scripts, the puppets and their little stage soon improved. After a hiatus of a few months in 1848, the puppet theater started back up again. Now there were seventeen puppets. By 1854 Maurice had a real puppet theater set up on the right-hand side of the parlor theater. The stage, with particularly ingenious mechanical engineering, let the puppets be manipulated in more and more complex ways. There were performances one after the other, as shown by Sand's notebook entitled "Archives of Maurice Sand's Puppet Theater" ["Archives du théâtre de marionnettes de Maurice Sand"]. All the productions were written down with the title, author, puppeteers, and date of the performance:

1854

April	*Oswald the Scotsman* (comedy)	Scenarios by Maurice Sand
	[*Oswald l'Ecossais*]	Interpreted by Maurice and Lambert
	Roccoforte (comedy)	
	Yseult de Vivonne (drama)	
	Elfrida the Jewess	
	[*Elfrida la juive*]	
14 August	*A Woman and an Overnight Bag* [*Une femme et un sac de nuit*] (comedy)	Scenarios par Maurice Interpreted by Maurice-Thiron(?)
15 August	*Richard XXII* (comedy)	

18 August	*Arthur I* (drama)	
20 August	*The Ruins of Niewsedel* [*Les ruines de Niewsedel*] (drama in 3 acts)	Scenarios by Maurice Interpreted by Maurice and Lambert
23 September	*Cucumber with a Hat* [*Combrillo di sombrero*] (drama in 2 acts)	
27 September	*The Green Bean Inn* [*L'Auberge du Haricot Vert*] (comedy)	Scenario by Maurice Interpreted by Maurice and Victor Borie

The puppet theater was inspired by the same things as the parlor theater and some of the plays produced in Paris: fantasy, the *commedia dell'arte*, Shakespeare, and Tirso de Molina. In this way the three kinds of theater, from the noblest to the simplest, from the most serious to the most comical, echoed back and forth and blended into one another. A dizzying carnival mirror of reality, the art of the *spectacle*, of illusion took on many forms. As Sand observed, "On stage the puppets obey the basic laws of theater. It is always the architectural temple, immense or microscopic, where desires and passions make their moves. There is no philosophical difference between the Grand-Opera and the puppet shows on the Champs-Elysées. Faust's Mephisto is the same Satan as Punch's devil with his little horns."[105]

Through the years the puppets grew in sophistication and number. While some were sculpting the heads of puppets needed for new scenarios, and others were working on costumes and props, one of the "workers" in this extraordinary studio would read to them out loud.[106] Maurice would whittle expressive little faces of men and women from the wood of a linden. Lambert would paint them, covering their heads with straw, horsehair, or real human hair; their eyes were two enamel tacks. Next they had to get the right costume for their sex and role. The attics of Nohant contain lots of big dressers with labels written in Sand's hand: "ribbons," "buttons," "headgear," "hats," and still others testify to the many kinds of sewing and tinkering projects under her supervision. She herself made "quite a few military uniforms, medieval costumes, and finally clothes to be worn at the court of Louis XV or XVI embroidered *ad hoc* in silk, chenille, gold or silver thread, and velvet" and felt "rightly proud" of the female puppets' undergarments, "chemises, slips, and ruffs of all sorts."[107]

Decors, props, furniture, nothing was left to chance in this miniature theater. The lighting required a lot of skill: the puppeteers' desire to represent day, night, the sun, the stars, the light of the moon, called for real technical genius. Balandard, the outspoken clown at the center of many scenarios, gradually turned into the main figure of the puppet shows. All around him were puppets representing all manner of social rank and position, aristocrats, bourgeois, servants, peasants, clerics, convicts, and some fantastic figures. Certain recurring characters had names, such as Captain Vachard, the fairy Azote, Brother Riboulard, and Sister Céleste; the stories were modified according to their appearances. A great many of the puppets are now on display in the stables of the château de Nohant.

JOYS, SORROWS, AND WORRIES

The 1840s were marked by music and the great figure of Chopin. Strong political convictions led Sand to take an active role in the initial phases of the Revolution of 1848. In the following decade, she did not abandon politics but retreated back into writing. The author of *François the Waif* was above all a strong voice for the opposition, criticizing, protesting, or encouraging in the press. The years of repression following "Louis-Napoleon's 18th Brumaire,"[108] as Karl Marx called it, scarcely allowed anything else.

Her life turned more toward all sorts of artistic, sewing, and tinkering projects. People with great talent or little worked together without giving a thought to any hierarchical organization of function or ability. With its in-house stage and puppet theater

Nohant became a fantastic workshop where each person could happily pursue his chosen activity. This was Sand's way of fulfilling her dream of a community of artists living together in peace and harmony.

Chopin left, then died. The man who came to share Sand's life was fourteen years her junior, scarcely older than Maurice, and like him a painter and engraver. In the household's daily activities he was another man, dynamic and hardworking, who soon came to be more of a husband to Sand than Chopin, who did nothing but music. Alexandre Manceau began managing Nohant, scrupulously carrying out his tasks, which were formerly the responsibility of Casimir, who did a pretty good job, selling a field here and buying a piece of land there, in order to streamline the estate.[109]

The enterprising young artist of course got involved in the theater activities: he acted and sometimes helped write the sketches; he managed the theater, setting up the ingenious stage-lighting and the ambitious decors for which he supervised, in the fall of 1856, the "carpenters, painters, and woodworkers, from morning till night."[110] An avid entomologist, he collected rare species and promptly got the whole family interested in caterpillars, butterflies, and insects. He drew two very beautiful portraits of Sand. She particularly liked the one he drew with a pencil that had once belonged to Thomas Couture.

He painstakingly recorded in a diary each day's activities and Sand's progress on plays and novels, often read aloud in the evening to the family and friends. When he was away, Sand stepped in for him, since she recognized the importance of this detailed register of everybody's activities, not just her own. The diaries read like a ship's log about life at Nohant and the comings and goings of all its inhabitants.

Manager and secretary, engraver and handyman, Manceau was discreet, but he was not self-effacing in his discretion. Wanting to maintain his financial independence, he kept on drawing and engraving,[111] which gave him an income that he meant to put to good use. Every year he exhibited at the Paris Salon, all the while working as a book illustrator; he occasionally engraved some of Maurice's drawings as illustrations for Sand's works. Sand said very little about this relationship, which seems to have very quickly found its footing. Yet it appears that the understanding between Alexandre and Aurore ("Manceau" and "Madame," as they decorously referred to each other in the diaries and their correspondence) was profound, as will be shown by the rest of the story.

The men that Sand loved all had a certain physical resemblance. In the drawings we have of them, they look fragile, slight, and a bit reserved, a little like Sand herself. Their age? Sand often repeated that she needed youthful enthusiasm to avoid sinking into bitterness and worry, even if that meant always being a bit, "by instinct and inclination,"[112] the mother of the men that she loved. As she recalled in *Story of My Life*, "I like daydreaming, meditation, and work; but beyond a certain point, I get gloomy because my thoughts turn somber, and if I'm forced to see reality in its sinister aspects, one of two things happens: either my soul surrenders or fun comes to the rescue. . . . I have an absolute need of true, healthy fun."[113]

Sand's maternal disposition, often evoked, was characterized by great generosity, unfailing devotion, exceptional foresight and provision, a certain taste for authority. In her intimate relationships, however, the word "child" seems most appropriate. Sand herself recognized this: "What can one do to gladden the hours that people spend together day after day? Talking politics generally keeps men busy, women like talking about clothes. I am neither man nor woman in that respect; I'm a child. While I'm working on something that delights my eyes or taking a walk that busies my legs, there has to be an exchange of vitality going on around me so that I don't feel the emptiness and horror of the human condition."[114]

Sand looked for men like her, children at heart no doubt, but children *like her*. With them she meant to live free, to create and travel, in a fine "exchange of vitality." That was the scenario for the beginning of her literary career with Jules Sandeau and her Berrichon friends, also the scenario she imagined in her *Traveler's Letters*, where she introduced herself as a "wandering schoolboy,"[115] delighted to be out and about as well as independent. This fantasy relationship with the opposite sex would stick with her for a long time.

It was the same old story with Manceau, and (almost) nothing had changed over the years. The young engraver was scarcely older than Chopin when he and Sand had met; he was the age of most of the men she had known up until then. Portrait of the lover as an eternally young man? "The individual named G[eorge] Sand"[116] must have (also) wanted Alexandre to become a brother, a chum, a fellow traveler, an artist, as she was.

Sand would walk with Manceau through the countryside. Since childhood she had been an excellent walker and loved hiking. Imported from England, this new leisure-time activity did not mean walking to get somewhere for some particular reason, to the fields or the next village to hire somebody or sell some livestock, but walking for the pleasure of being out in the open and enjoying the landscape. Local tourism was starting up and changing the way people looked at rural life. Sometimes with a carriage following behind, often with a guest, Sand and her companion would walk to villages around Nohant, to Briantes, Sarzay, Saint-Chartier, Neuvy-Saint-Sépulchre, La Motte-Feuilly, Sainte-Sévère, and also to Crevant and the lead mines at Urciers.

They would admire a village sitting high on a hill, a chateau, or a particularly "picturesque" farm, then visit a Romanesque church with its frescoes or some natural curiosity. Eugène Grandsire, another of Maurice's painter friends, sketched "Madame" in her walking costume, a long dress buttoned up to the neck and a broad-brimmed hat with an ample veil to protect her face from insects as well as the sun.[117] We also have a few drawings of their excursions in the valley of the Creuse, later published in *Le Monde Illustré*.

During the summer of 1857 the hikers discovered the Creuse valley and the little village of Gargilesse, "which, in this season, is a paradise on earth."[118] As she wrote to Maurice, then away in Paris,

We just got back [to Nohant] this evening, not too tired, despite ten some leagues [around forty kilometers] on foot in two days under a tropical sun, proof being that Manceau caught an African butterfly and another from the south of France, Algira and

Gordius. . . . From Châteaubrun to Gargilesse there is a lovely walk along the banks of the Creuse. Four hours of bushwhacking, that's quite a lot. . . . It's an enchanting area and one that had remained unknown to us, despite all the walking we do. . . . I was really sorry you weren't there, but we're fantasizing about a little cottage there.[119]

By May of the next year it was a done deal. With his savings Manceau bought a tiny house that Sand laughingly called "Villa Algira" or "Villa Manceau." It had two little rooms, one upstairs and one down with steep open stairs in between, a cellar, a huge sloping roof, and a miniscule garden, also with a stiff slope. Meals were taken at the nearby inn, and they merrily made the best of the humblest furnishings: "The little house consisting of two exceedingly clean rooms, iron bedsteads, straw-bottomed chairs with whitewood tables is attached to other houses that look just the same but less clean, lived in by local peasants. . . . For them I'm not the lady of the manor, but an Auvergnate, neither male nor female, meaning *a stranger who is not from here*, but who likes being here all the same."[120]

While Sand worked in the little room reserved for her, her companion shared his interest in insects with the village children: "We're in Gargilesse, my Bouli, and the weather isn't good. . . . Fortunately the little house is well sealed and very livable, no matter the weather, and I work inside when it rains. . . . All the children are out looking for caterpillars and often turn up with interesting things. Manceau classifies them and gives out rewards according to the find, nothing if the caterpillar hasn't been brought in fresh and healthy wrapped in a leaf, nothing if it's ordinary. One fine day the whole village will be part of the Entomology Society."[121]

Manceau spared no effort to make his "little house" comfortable and to accommodate guests if necessary. As Sand observed, once again in a letter to Maurice,

There's no way to stop him from fixing his place up much more for our benefit than for his. He's turning it into a ship's cabin and measuring each centimeter so that everybody will have his own gear, nail, pot, a place for each boot, etc., etc. . . . So he indulges his two passions, dedication and doodads. I say this to console myself for seeing him so stubbornly spending his meager profits. . . . I'll have you know that Manceau went for a swim in the Creuse. . . . On Sundays everybody's in the water, swimming and fishing. Little kids and some of the women go swimming too. Here the women work more than the men, more big differences *from things in our neck of the woods.*[122]

Sand greatly enjoyed this new kind of dwelling and the customs of this rugged area so different from Nohant. "This higgledy-piggledy village life in all its true *rusticity* strikes me as much more normal than life in a château,"[123] she declared to Solange. She and Manceau would often go to Gargilesse for short visits. *Walks Around a Village* [*Promenades autour d'un village*] came out in 1859 along with the illustrated edition of the rustic novels.[124] There she described her walking tours in the area and the discoveries to which they led, also commenting on the new vogue for picturesque rural scenes and the debates about realism, a new and fashionable aesthetic: "Today art loves and sees everything naïve, even a broken-down wheelbarrow with an urn lying on its side makes for a painting on the blond manure where a rooster is strutting proudly as though on a purple carpet. . . . As for me, feeling that everything depends on the artist, that is all I can understand about the word 'realism.'"[125]

Maurice was still a bachelor. Sand had hoped he would marry his cousin Augustine Brault, but to no avail. After that she kept watch, often urging her son not "to fall for"[126] some pretty little face in Paris and trying to get art dealers interested in his drawings, engravings, and paintings. "Come back as soon as you can. That's my refrain,"[127] she never failed to write as soon as he left Nohant. "Bouli" endeavored to make his mark, but without any great results. He tried for a government commission, copying paintings, if need be, and sent work to the Salons. Delacroix, who was known not to look out much for his students, seemed indifferent to him, which

Maurice regretted; and his mother appealed to Delacroix "most urgently,"[128] but apparently without much success. In 1855, when both Manceau and Lambert were showing work at the Salon that was part of the first Universal Exhibition in Paris, Maurice felt discouraged: none of his pieces had been accepted. Sand urged him to persevere and be patient.

Her letters to her friends did not hide that she was eager to find a wife for her "dear darling."[129] She was looking for "a *good-hearted* girl, happy to be a bit spoiled, and endowed with the means to enlarge the family one day."[130] With Jules Boucoiran, who had been Maurice's tutor, she got down to brass tacks in February 1857:

> Maurice has decided to get married, and he's looking for a wife. He hasn't yet met the right one, and I'm asking you, . . . who have taught the best young people around, if you know of an eligible party who would suit him in mind and means.
>
> Here's his financial situation. When he marries, I can give him a dowry of 200,000 f. of good land. His father promises him a dowry of 50,000 f. . . . After I'm gone, Nohant will provide at least 200,000 f. to be split between Maurice and his sister. Plus, my literary estate represents a very good source of capital. After M. Dudevant's death, there will also be more than 100,000 f. (he says) to be split.
>
> . . . Maurice's . . . painting also brings in some cash and guarantees him a living. . . . He is nice, as you know, sensible, never having been in trouble, a good son, and sure to be a good father, for he adores children. . . . He's thirty-three at this point, but nobody wants to believe it, since he looks so young.
>
> If you know of a young person who more or less meets these conditions, with a pleasant face, good and reliable character, domestic inclinations . . . plus the appropriate means . . . , Maurice would pay you a visit. We don't much care about the family's status and business, as long as they come by their wealth honorably and the parents don't require long stays far from Paris . . . and far from me, as all summer long I'll provide bed, board, all the comforts and indulgences that it is nice to give one's children. . . .

[Maurice] is healthy, and he has a fine pedigree. His future
wife would have to have good blood as well so that we could
hope for fine, adorable children.[131]

How far removed these calculations are from the novels where
love bursts upon the scene in one fell swoop for two penniless
youngsters who are a perfect match in heart and spirit!

When two years later she learned that Maurice had fallen in
love with a girl of sixteen, Sand asked Émile Aucante to make
inquiries about her parents, affluent merchants in rue Poissonnière
in Paris. Despite Maurice's wish to marry "a very young woman,"
she was apprehensive about the girl's "irresolute character."[132] Sand
had already entered into all kinds of financial arrangements when
she learned that Clothilde's parents were not married. Then all
the wedding planning ground to a halt.[133] In keeping with the etiquette of her time, Sand acted like an aristocrat with an inheritance
to protect, something that she nevertheless tried to forget, and
something that she condemned in her books as well. Without any
hesitation she claimed the right to intervene in the personal affairs
of the man to whom she had given her name. "[Maurice] is always
my steadfast consolation,"[134] she liked to say again and again.

The little community of Nohant was then mainly men. Sand
managed everybody's activities, sleeping in the morning, sewing or
walking in the afternoon, composing sketches and reading aloud
to others in the evening when there wasn't some kind of performance. At the end of the evening she would retire to her room on
the second floor to write to an ever greater number of correspondents and to continue the novel abandoned the night before. The
house grew quiet, darkness enveloped the garden, and there was
no sound from the handful of cottages in the village of Nohant.
Manceau would have prepared what she needed: paper, trimmed
pens, blue ink, cigarette paper, tobacco, and a glass of sugar water.
By candlelight and then oil lamps Sand would start writing with
the amazingly single-minded concentration that she always seems
to have possessed. For her, writing did not compete with living her
life; she had no need to choose one over the other, like Balzac and

later on Flaubert. Creation seems to have been the high point of the day, and Sand made it go on a good part of the night.

Since 1832 she had been writing very fast, always "all fired up"[135] from her last novel, sometimes saying there was "no longer time to eat and sleep"[136] when the newspaper was expecting the next installment or the publisher the corrected proof. Even so, she did not just write down whatever entered her head, without correcting or crossing things out, as some critics readily maintained, eager to contend that she carried on in a typically feminine way.[137] In fact, her archived manuscripts show numerous corrections, with whole passages rewritten or thrown out, with chapters sometimes revised or substantially changed. Suggestions from close friends, advice from publishers as to titles, chapter divisions, or the length of the entire piece also led to all kinds of revisions. There is nothing "natural" about Sand's writing; it was instead the result of constant and considerable work along with a remarkable mastery of the whole production process, from the manuscript to the book.

In May 1856, "with a hand broken and cramped with exhaustion,"[138] she managed to change her penmanship by patiently doing exercises for weeks on end. She adopted an "up and down" style that allowed her to write "much faster without too many smears"[139] and to estimate more accurately the number of printed pages her manuscripts would yield, which was the subject of endless calculations in her correspondence with publishers. While she was "killing herself with work,"[140] she would sometimes dream of giving up writing for walking, gardening, or reading. As she wrote to Pierre Bocage in 1854, "I confess that books don't give me half the pleasure the spade does and that I'd like to have money or no responsibilities, which would amount to the same thing. Then I'd like to forget that I was once an author and plunge into living in the body, with an inner life of daydreams, contemplation, and a bit of reading of my choice . . . . That's my dream."[141] A while later she acknowledged: "I always want to be somewhere else. For me, that means a little place where I would get a rest from all my dealings, every worry, every boring relationship, every domestic problem, all responsibility for my own existence."[142] From then on, writing novels sometimes felt like a limitation on her personal freedom, the need to earn enough for the whole household yoking her to endless, exhausting work.

Sand was earning quite a bit of money.[143] Her land brought in relatively little (between 7,000 and 9,000 francs a year, some 10,000 euros), but she earned substantial income from her novels, essays, and articles in the press, their republication in book form and many reeditions in all sorts of formats, plus the performance of her plays. With Balzac and Hugo, she was one of the best-paid authors of her time, although Eugène Sue remained at the top of the list for a long time.

Yet she had lots of expenses and few savings. As she confessed in a letter to the banker Édouard Rodrigues, "I've spent my whole life never gratifying myself, writing when I would have preferred to dream, staying put when I would have preferred running around, sordidly scrimping on certain totally personal needs, certain luxurious bathrobes and slippers . . . ; not indulging my guests' taste for fine food, not going to theaters, concerts, art exhibits, living like a hermit, even though I love life's hustle and bustle and traveling around."[144] Maintaining a huge household at Nohant with the help of several servants for the kitchen, house, garden, and stables, Sand was always ready to feed anyone who showed up and sometimes welcomed friends, their spouses, and children for several days or weeks at a time. In Paris she kept a pied-à-terre with a yearly lease, first at 3 rue Racine, then at 97 rue des Feuillantines (now rue Claude-Bernard), that the widow Martine looked after. In addition to supporting Maurice, who had his own servant, and her daughter, to whom she paid an allowance, she also provided for Augustine Bertholdi's household, paid for the services of her agent Émile Aucante, and gave generously to old friends and needy inhabitants of Nohant.

Her endless negotiations with publishers, with all their discussions, hassles, and disagreements, are the clearest proof of the close eye she kept on her income. She painstakingly championed high standards of work[145] and also worried about getting a good return on her literary capital. In her eyes, the main object of money was to assure one's independence and to allow for all sorts of generosity. In her novels, no matter what her character's class or status might be, every one of them got money by honest means and never failed to discuss its relative importance. Money was meant to be earned, then shared, spent for the common good, and not socked away. Nor was it to be the driving force of existence, as it was for Balzac, who saw money as the "only modern God."[146]

The birth of little Jeanne in 1849 brought Solange back closer to her mother. The relationship between mother and daughter picked up again bit by bit, but not without wariness on both their parts. As Sand wrote to Pierre-Jules Hetzel, "My daughter showed up out of the blue last Friday, and she left this morning. She came alone with her daughter and maid, embraced me tenderly enough but with too much composure, neither giving me nor asking for any word of explanation about the past. . . . I was unnaturally cool and severe with her. She was more submissive and contained than usual: frivolous and underhanded, loving no one and a heart totally devoid of conscience. . . . Besides that, quite gracious and silver-tongued for the moment . . . , not good, alas! no, not at all."[147]

A few letters were exchanged after Solange went back to Paris, and Sand even ventured to encourage her daughter to write.[148] "I wonder," she nevertheless noted, "if [Solange] is not a dream . . . , the shadow of something to which I thought I gave birth, but half remained in the world of dreams."[149] In the spring of 1852, Solange's relationship with her husband, "each one being as unfair and faithless as the other,"[150] showed signs of indubitable deterioration, even if they had both turned their attention elsewhere. Solange and Jeanne came to stay at Nohant several times in the following months. In August Solange left her daughter with Sand for a few weeks so that she could take care of some pressing matters. The vivacity of little "Nini," the way she clowned around while helping with the gardening or learning to embroider delighted her grandmother and the people close to her. Anxious to spare the little girl her parents' quarrels and dissipated lifestyle, Sand soon envisaged getting legal custody, thereby repeating her grandmother's gesture toward her.

In December 1854 the couple officially separated. Irritated to see his mother-in-law's influence on his wife and daughter, the sculptor put the child in a Parisian boarding school while the court decided her fate. When Sand was officially awarded custody a few days later, tragedy struck. During the night of 13–14 January 1855 Jeanne died of scarlet fever. She was not yet six. The diary reads:

> Sunday 14 January [written in Manceau's hand]. . . . Around ten [in the evening] an express messenger from Châteauroux brought a telegram announcing that poor little Nini's suffering had come to an end. . . . Madame is devastated and so is everybody else.
>
> Monday 15 [written in George Sand's hand]. A dead day. I went twice to the cemetery, first to mark out the grave and then to see if it was ready. . . . I talked with Maurice who is terribly demoralized by all these sorrows. Manceau left this morning for Châteauroux . . . where he'll wait for Solange and *Nini*![151]

On 17 January Sand wrote to Adolphe Lemoine-Montigny: "My friend . . . , I'm making a great effort to write to you. Yesterday, alongside my grandmother and my father, we buried our dear little Jeanne, who died at her boarding school of poorly treated scarlet fever and in the wake of six months of malaise and perhaps grief. . . . I won't say how dreadful I'm feeling. . . . Anyway, today I just couldn't find the words. It has made my poor daughter a bit crazy. . . . Maurice is shattered. . . . Manceau's heart is broken, like mine; he so loved this little girl, waiting on her hand and foot like a *maid*!"[152]

Sand drew a number of portraits of the little girl from memory, the only remaining souvenirs of her existence. All winter long, "ill with a great sorrow,"[153] she expressed her deep pain to her correspondents and retraced the unspeakable attitude of her son-in-law whom she held responsible for Jeanne's death. "I had arranged my life for *her*," she wrote to Ida Dumas, "and it's hard to take it back for my own use."[154] In Paris Solange tried to distract her pain in the social whirl, regularly sending her mother juicy reports about her dinners and evening parties, without mentioning the names of the men swirling around a very pretty young woman, the daughter of a very famous woman.

On 11 March 1855 Sand, along with Maurice and Manceau, left Nohant for a "little jaunt through Italy"[155] until the end of May. Keeping a close eye on expenses at Nohant, she left precise orders with Sylvain Brunet, her coachman:

> Keep 1 rooster and 12 young hens. No more than one bushel of grain per month.
>
> Get bran bread in La Châtre for Jacques [a manservant].
>
> If the puppy follows old Marie, let her go, but if she sticks around the house, give her away.
>
> Give Henri [Sylvain's brother] the keys to the winepress, cellar, storage room, haylofts, and bakery.
>
> Don't do any laundry. If you need a few dish towels or cleaning rags, Henri's mother will wash them, and I'll pay her.
>
> Don't fire up the ovens.
>
> When the tenant farmers bring in their cartloads, I'll pay them. They won't be fed since there won't be any cooking while I'm away. . . .
>
> Tell Henri to hitch up the climbing vine in the garden with the poles cut from the little grove. . . . He should turn over the rest of the garden plots and seed them with alfalfa and oats.[156]

And so on and so forth. This time, she was headed to Rome, first taking the train to Marseilles, then after some visits in that area, they would go by sea to Genoa, Livorno, Pisa, finally Civitavecchia. On 19 March they reached the Eternal City. The painter Gustave Boulanger who was staying at the Villa Medicis gave them a tour of Rome. Sand's first impressions were not very positive. As she wrote to Solange, "The first day here was a great disillusion for us. The road from the sea to Rome's gates is a dreadful desert. The modern city is so ugly compared with the old part that you first think you've been fooled, since the old city, all hemmed in and smothered by the new constructions, is at first invisible."[157]

When Maurice fell ill, she soon decided to leave Rome for the countryside, namely, Frascati: "Since Rome is the hugest and most tiresome thing in the world to visit and look at, and life odious in a room at an inn, we left the splendors of Holy Week just when the whole universe was rushing in. We've found a place in Frascati . . . , for a modest price the ground floor of the Piccolomini villa. A palace, no less, but what a palace! Frescoes everywhere and no furniture anywhere, quite a lot of fleas, in short, this part of Italy and Majorca are much the same."[158] They started sightseeing again, but to no avail. Sand loved traveling through the beautiful Roman countryside with mountains off in the distance—as she wrote, "It's paradise"[159]—but she did not have much taste for ruins, palaces, museums, and churches:

> It's curious, beautiful, interesting, amazing, but it's too dead. . . . You'd have to live inside it all, with concentration of mind, fantastic memory, and extinguished imagination. . . . When you've spent several days looking at urns, tombs, crypts, columbaria, you long to get out a bit and set your eyes on nature. But in Rome nature means torrents of rain that go on and on until all of a sudden there's overwhelming heat and bad air. The city is foul with ugliness and filth! It is La Châtre, only a hundred times bigger; for it's immense and decorated with old and new monuments that knock you over the head at every step, without giving you an ounce of pleasure, since they're all smothered and spoiled by heaps of misshapen and wretched buildings.[160]

On this last point she was not alone: most of the French visitors at that time noted the papal city's deplorable neglect. On 23 April Maurice, Manceau, and Sand took a carriage to Florence and started sightseeing again. "A pleasant stay for people who like cities," observed Sand, who nevertheless appreciated that Florence was "completely civilized,"[161] a welcome contrast from Rome. Next they went by train to Lucca and La Spezia, "a tranquil and lovely spot, . . . very good for walking":[162] "Today we're out and about in the countryside, tramping through ravines and climbing all over without getting our feet wet. I'm sitting on some warm sandy soil covered with flowers; more white heather, superb wild orchids, rosemary, and a host of other superb plants whose names I don't know."[163]

It is clear that "Madame" continued to prefer the beautiful countryside and the great outdoors to the cities with all their churches and museums—her impression of Rome was still lingering on.[164] In Genoa Maurice, who made a number of drawings of the trip, left Manceau and his mother for Milan. The two of them took a boat to Marseilles, then the train to Paris where they spent a few days seeing old friends. Sand wanted to look elegant and asked her maid to send her "gray- and violet-striped watered silk dress with the bodice and one or two embroidered collars to wear with this high-necked dress."[165] They returned to Nohant on 29 May.

As soon as the travelers were back home, they set to work with even greater intensity, having lots of projects under way: articles, novels, and plays. In August Sand briefly entertained a few guests, including Sylviane Arnould-Plessy, a famous actress who was the mistress of Prince Jérôme Napoléon, a young actress named Bérengère (she had played in *The Winepress*) as well as Émile de Girardin, recently widowed.

The following summer Solange, "terribly ill,"[166] spent several weeks at Nohant. Distressed to see the state her daughter was in, Sand briefly considered taking her to the waters, then changed her mind. After growing suspicions and a few sharp exchanges, their relationship was once again fraught. Soon Sand accused Solange of slandering her in front of old friends. "My world's worst enemy is my daughter. How jolly!"[167] she wrote to Émile Aucante. When Solange told her mother about her money problems, Sand replied:

Here I am fifty-five years old, and I can no longer renew the strength that nature will no doubt soon refuse me. I've got no investments; it was never possible to save anything. I'd have had to retire into a little corner and live absolutely alone, never going out and putting money aside. . . . You should live simply or learn to work. To anything anyone ever says to you, you reply that it's impossible. So what do you want me to come up with for you, poor child? . . . My only advice is this: both privation and work require a strong will, and when you say *how boring*, I've got nothing more to say.[168]

In the 1850s the business and vicissitudes of her private life found a greater echo in Sand's novels. Two of her novels were directly inspired by the theater of Nohant, *The Castle in the Wilderness*, published in 1851, and *The Snowman* [*L'homme de neige*], published in 1859. The second, appearing in installments in the *Revue des Deux Mondes*, signaled Sand's reconciliation with its director, François Buloz. Dedicated to Maurice, the novel takes place in Sweden at the end of the eighteenth century—Sand did some required reading on the subject, just enough to sprinkle the tale with bits of "local color." The protagonist of this novel is a young puppeteer named Christian Waldo, and it is an ideal way to show off everything that can be done with these "little actors."[169]

Attentive to the problems of blended families, Sand treated the difficulties of relationships across the generations, between mothers, daughters, and adoptive daughters in other novels in the same period—for example, in *Mont-Revêche*, in 1853, and *The Goddaughter* [*La filleule*], which came out as a book the same year. For a time she had stopped dreaming of utopian families, showing instead the odd misadventures of demanding young women and distraught fathers and mothers.

Written after Sand returned from Italy, *La Daniella* was published in 1857. A blend of diary and letters sprinkled with Italian words,[170] the novel recounts the adventures of a young painter in Rome, Jean Valreg. In some respects, it is the exact opposite of Germaine de Staël's *Corinne ou L'Italie*, which had appeared some fifty years earlier. The criticism of the way the Papal States were governed is much harsher, and the book shows singularly lukewarm enthusiasm for Rome and its ruins.[171] Very much opposed to Napoléon III's support of the pope, Sand, who was friends with Mazzini and Garibaldi, had no desire to keep quiet about the papal administration's neglect, the prelates' arrogance, and the great economic and spiritual poverty of Rome's inhabitants. As Victor Hugo wrote to her from Guernsey, "*Daniella* is a great and beautiful book. . . . I won't discuss the politics of it, for the only things I could write about Italy would be impossible to read in France, and they'd probably prevent my letter from reaching you. I'm talking to you, an artist, about the work of art; as for the great aspirations to liberty and progress, they are ineffably part of your nature, and poetry like yours is always a breath of the future. The revolution is light, and what are you if not a lantern?"[172]

Everybody did not have the same opinion, far from it. Political divisions, of course, surfaced in the many critiques of the novel's political and aesthetic ideas. Concerned about the tone Sand dared take vis-à-vis a country allied with France, the minister of the interior sent a warning to *La Presse*, the newspaper publishing *La Daniella* in installments. A year later Sand would openly support the cause of Italian reunification by publishing two articles, "The War" ["La guerre"] and "Garibaldi," that would later circulate as brochures.

After a novel in the form of a dialogue between peasants and animals, *The Devil Afield* [*Le diable aux champs*], and a fantasy novel, *The Green Ladies* [*Les dames vertes*], Sand in 1858 published an excellent novel set during the reign of Louis XIII and reflecting that period's mind-set, *The Handsome Gentlemen of Gilded-Wood* [*Les beaux messieurs de Bois-Doré*], which mainly takes place at the château of Briantes, near Nohant. As Sand explained to Charles-Edmond, "Historical novels promise serious things, important characters, narratives of great events. That's not what I'm doing. . . . I'm working from my point of view, and I've tried hard to be historically accurate down to the slightest details about the time's customs, ideas, and manners. Everything in my fable is rigorously exact."[173]

This was a rare undertaking for Sand, whose novels could assume a remarkable number of different shapes. Drawing a living portrait of the condition of workers in the paper and cutlery industry in the city of Thiers, *The Black City* [*La ville noire*] appeared in 1861, the same year as *Le marquis de Villemer*. After the novels of social commitment of the 1840s and the rustic novels,

Sand managed to work other forms and subjects into her novels, always with great creative energy and invention. Was she a realist? Obviously, that label does not seem to fit either her work or the work of the young authors of the time, as she explained to Ernest Feydeau, who had just sent her his novel *Fanny*, "People have taken upon themselves to baptize your way of writing and Flaubert's as realism, I don't know why. . . . Calling it realism isn't right because art is complex, infinite. The artist creates reality in himself, his own reality, and not anybody else's."[174]

She had already made similar remarks, in particular to Champfleury, and they would resurface again and again in the following years. Above and beyond her desire to define a very personal relationship to art and the reality it tries to render, Sand showed great liberty in her fiction, moving with ease from novels of social commitment to fantasy novels, from historical novels to novels analyzing family relationships, or to novels drawing on all these different types. Her narrative bag of tricks was characterized by the amazing composite of genres she would illustrate throughout her career, endlessly modifying the settings, milieus, time periods of her characters, and recycling old letters and diaries in ways that suited her particularly well.

Often preferring the first person, she brought the writing of novels and letters closer together, and the many articles that she continued to publish frequently took the form of open letters. From that point on, the artist's *approach* seemed less constrained by distinctions between literary genres. No matter what kind of text she wrote, the approach was immediately and unmistakably hers.

FAMILY AFFAIRS

Physically, George Sand had changed. In January 1853, nearing the age of forty-nine, she announced to Pierre-Jules Hetzel "her climacteric," "exhausting bouts of sweating,"[175] and constant fatigue. Her slim silhouette had turned stocky, her face was thicker, and her hair was gray in spots. Pencil drawings, pastels, lithographs, and portraits in ink and watercolors throughout the volumes of her letters show sure signs of age. Except for an occasional remark about her stamina, considerable up to that point, she did not seem to attach much importance to all this, continuing "to laugh and race around the countryside *like a youngster*."[176]

In Paris on her way back from Italy, she ordered a corset with "much more substantial stays"[177] than those she had originally planned. She bundled herself more tightly, squeezing her bulges and concealing her extra pounds in more voluminous, high-collared dresses without much of a waist, in keeping with current fashion. Sand no longer showed her arms, shoulders, or cleavage. Trousers were fine for youth, with all its whims and yearnings for independence. Now independence was in her head and pen. Her wardrobe, on the other hand, had become as staid as could be.

Now Sand gave more thought to her wardrobe. Everything required careful consideration, the material, the color, the cut of the dress to be made, any decoration such as lace, guipure, braid, or embroidery. Solange in particular was entrusted with her shopping in Paris, and Sand would say precisely what she wanted, for example: "I'm choosing . . . on your recommendation, . . . the little gray- and black-striped material at 8 f. a meter, wide bolt, from the Chevaux Aubertot shop. Send me what I need, and then a bit more in case of accident, of the gray silk for the bodice lining, plus the velvet for the trim, and in your letter draw me a little sketch of the look you recommend."[178] Another example: "The swatch I'm sending you is from the shop on the Chaussée d'Antin. It costs around 56 f. for 12 meters. But I find it's a bit dark. But if you think it's good, that's fine with me. In this lot I really liked the material with the yellow and black checks. . . . Don't forget the lining. . . . The reason for this dress is to have something very simple for mornings in Paris, or in town if I'm on a trip."[179]

On 27 October 1852, in his studio on quai de l'Horloge in Paris, the photographer Pierre-Amboise Richebourg welcomed the author and her son, Maurice, who had come to have themselves "daguerreotyped." On 6 December the portraits arrived in Nohant: "We have received the photographs of Madame," Manceau noted in the diary, "but they're so horribly ugly we threw everything in the fire. Memory is more faithful than such realities."[180] A tough lesson to see oneself for the first time "as she really was," after so many portraits done by artists, major and minor!

Sand thought she had destroyed these portraits,[181] but she was not reckoning with the specifics of the new invention of photography, first appearing in 1839, or with the intervention of Félix Nadar, engraver, illustrator, and brilliant jack-of-all-trades. Ten years later, one of the portraits destroyed in the past resurfaced. In his huge studio in the boulevard des Capucines, Nadar salvaged Richebourg's proofs.[182] He chose one, printed it out, then did some revisions. Next he printed the portrait in a visiting card format and put them up for sale. Sand was a celebrity, as he had known for a long time,[183] and this guaranteed the success of the operation. When Sand received letters asking her to sign this daguerreotype that she thought to have destroyed, she was flabbergasted. Despite Nadar's photo editing, she hardly looks her best: in a black dress with a white lace collar, her body jammed down in chair, she turns a glum eye to the camera. She soon contacted Nadar and set a date for a new sitting.

On 4 and 5 March 1864 Sand went to Nadar's studio and returned on 9 March. For these sittings—very long at that time, given the exposure time for collodion plates—she wore three different outfits: a dress of black watered silk with braid, a plaid dress with a lacy bow at the neck, and a black- and white-striped dress with a burnoose-like collar. She sported lovely gold pendant earrings, and her hair was crimped with a curling iron, with a very visible part down the middle. In her striped dress Sand posed more than twenty times, by turns standing, with her elbow on a column, sitting full face, partially turned away, or in profile. Substantially retouched—Nadar erased the shadows under her eyes and her wrinkles, smoothed out the neck and the lower chin—these portraits were widely distributed, first in visiting card format, sometimes with Sand's signature, and later as postcards. "My children are delighted by my photos, and they thank you for having taken them," Sand wrote to Nadar on 24 March 1864. "So destroy Richebourg's dreadful photograph."[184]

A little while later Nadar drew a playful lithograph glorifying Sand, who had become a true friend of his. Around one of the photo portraits he had just taken, he arranged seven vignettes summarizing her life as one often sees in a traditional representation of the lives of the saints.[185] The eighth vignette forms a broad banner at the bottom of the lithograph and bears the title "In the armchairs of the French Academy." Sand's novels are piled on the chairs of the bicorn-bearing Academicians who look obviously stunned by this "occupation."

When they were not talking about clothes, the relationship between Solange and her mother remained difficult. The young woman never failed to ask for money. Sand suspected that she was carrying on an expensive affair with one of the young men always hovering around her. When Solange informed her of her plans to visit Nohant, even to move to Berry, Sand gave her this categorical reply:

> I am against . . . your coming here in September or October. I feel and want to feel too much antipathy for certain people you've mentioned, and I have no desire to see them together with you. . . . The same goes for your attempting to buy property near me, and if you're going to Châteauroux for that reason, I urge you to drop the idea for your own good. I am no fan of *surprises*. . . . I mean not *to know* how you arrange your private life, and to keep it that way, I do not want you living anywhere near Nohant.[186]

After that letter Solange decided to break things off completely with her mother. Sand nevertheless went on paying her allowance until October 1865 when her fears became firm beliefs: Solange was selling her favors. As she explained to Charles Poncy,

> If [Solange] were just flirtatious, fickle, seductive, or whimsical, I would scold her and put up with the harm she's doing herself. But she is no madcap, but rather a depraved soul. She's sleeping around and taking money for it. . . . She has an allowance of

3,000 francs and she doesn't work. . . . She needs at least 20,000 francs a year to live as she does; where does she get the money? Now I know only too well what everybody knows. . . . As for me, I don't tolerate prostitution, and it's all over between me and a person who has gone down that road, laughing, holding her head up high, with . . . a name she ought to have respected and enough money to lead a quiet, studious, and ordinary life with dignity.[187]

Sand judged her daughter's life by her own life's measure. While she was very free in her romantic involvements, she never wanted to depend on anyone for money. Quite the other way around, the men that she loved lived, in part, off money earned by Sand. She had never been able to conceive of anything aside from a relationship between artists who shared their creative endeavors, in literature, music, or painting, making for some kind of equality in her eyes and guaranteeing similar tastes. Solange's behavior struck her as altogether common, cowardly, and immoral. The two women would remain on bad terms for a long time: Sand held her tongue; her daughter went abroad.[188]

With her son things were very different. In March 1861 Maurice was awarded the Legion of Honor.[189] He was about to turn thirty-seven. Thanks to his mother, he was proud to be friends with Prince Jérôme. After a brief stay in Algeria, on 23 June he boarded the prince's yacht and headed for America. "I'm shushing all the frailties of a mother's heart,"[190] Sand wrote to him before worrying about how much the trip would cost. After Spain, Portugal, the Azores, and Newfoundland, they arrived in New York on 28 July:

Your letters inspire me with calm and courage. What a lot of things you'll wind up seeing! and what things to tell me! I don't much like the fog you wander around in for five or six days at a time! Well, there has to be some of that in your travel adventures! What a collection of memories for you, and I hope you're keeping a diary, so that you can remember them in order and give me a clear account of everything. I am following you on a map, but how much nicer it will be when you're here to show me your route.[191]

On 12 October Maurice was back in Nohant, "bright-eyed and bushy-tailed, after a little jaunt of more than 6,000 leagues," while Sand declared herself *"utterly overcome with relief."*[192] Having taken his mother's advice, Maurice had kept a diary and upon his return launched into writing up his adventures. *Six Thousand Leagues at Full Steam* [*Six mille lieues à toute vapeur*] was published in 1862 by Michel Lévy, with a preface by Sand.

The joint artistic endeavors got going again with renewed vigor, and their interest in botany, entomology, and mineralogy sent them on endless hikes in the surrounding countryside. Sand found a new adoptive son in Alexandre Dumas fils, a young and talented playwright who soon began participating in the parlor theater sketches and working with her on adapting some novels to the stage. He also acted some parts, and each time this "pretty, pretty child"[193] set out for Paris, Sand would call him back to Nohant. She added to her phalanstery of artists the young Édouard Cadol, who was starting out as a playwright, and the painter Charles Marchal, twenty-one years her junior, who left a lovely pencil portrait of Sand dated 1861. As she wrote to Alexandre Dumas fils, "Marchal makes me happy. We have the tenderest of feelings for each other, now I'm *his cousin*, God knows why. I call him *my darling*. But this evening we quarreled. He threatened to break my glasses, and I retorted that I'd make him eat them, and he's very funny, very entertaining, and basically very good-hearted, excellent."[194] This sounds more like a puppet show than some confession about an affair. Did Sand really feel anything more than rather exuberant affection for the painter, a sentiment she often evoked in comic mode? Did she later become his mistress?[195] Maybe the artist who was photographed at the time by Bingham in a flattering pose, with mustache and goatee, his left hand on the lapel of his jacket, managed to win her love.

In any case, she continued to surround herself with young men, big children whom she appreciated because they were funny, talented, and loved being alive. True, she made Augustine de Bertholdi her adoptive daughter, if not as a substitute for her own daughter; she was fond of the young actress Bérengère, whom she took traveling, and Marie Caillaud, who showed real talent as an actress, even though she worked as a maid, but Sand continued to prefer the company of men: none of these women was really an artist, and none possessed that rollicking good humor that only "the guys" enjoy together.

Soon thereafter Sand's joy knew no bounds. On 17 May 1862 Maurice was married! At the age of thirty-nine he wed the daughter of the engraver Luigi Calamatta, Lina, who was twenty. The families had known each other for a long time, given that the artist had engraved one of Sand's portraits years before, and everything was quickly arranged. The father, of rather modest means, would spend six months a year with his daughter at Nohant. The bride and groom seemed delighted with each other.

Nadar did their portrait. Maurice, who was going gray, sported a bow tie, with a gold watch chain conspicuously decorating his waistcoat, making him look more like a country squire than a puppeteer; Lina, leaning on a little pedestal table, *grassotta*, with a head of full, dark hair and prominent eyes, struck the nonchalant pose of the good child that everybody wanted her to be. Her future mother-in-law wrote: "The child is a purebred little Roman, *nera, nera,* as the song goes, frizzy, darling, clever, with a charming voice, a classic physiognomy. She is lovable and sincere; I'm just crazy about her. Of all the girls we've seen, she's the one I liked best. . . . At last, the future is smiling at us."[196]

The following July all of Sand's wishes were fulfilled. As she wrote to Alexandre Dumas fils, "Marc Antoine Sand was born this morning, on Bastille Day. He is big and strong, and he gazed at me carefully, deliberately as I gathered him up all warm and cozy in my apron. . . . We put him in a bath of Bordeaux wine where he wriggled around happy as could be. This evening he is nursing voraciously, and his nurse, none other than his little mother, is happy as a lark. . . . Papa Maurice cried like a baby and so did Papa Calamatta at the sight of the sturdy little brat."[197]

Family, the role of women, maternal feeling? On these points Sand had often expressed views, and she recognized how traditional they were: "Women can certainly, at given times, fill a social and political role with inspiration, but not a function that deprives them of their natural mission: the love of family. People have often told me my ideal of progress was backward, and there is no doubt that in the matter of progress the imagination can welcome all kinds of things. But is the heart destined to change? I don't think so, and I see women as forever slaves to their own hearts and innards. I've written that time and time again, and I'm still of the same opinion."[198]

There is no denying that Sand was fiercely attached to the ideal of equality between men and women, but apparently more for herself and the protagonists of her novels. For that matter, she never drew a line, as did, for instance, Marie d'Agoult, between femininity and the "natural mission" of motherhood. Sand considered feminine attributes, both good and bad, as essences that she saw (partially) lacking in herself, a novelist writing under a man's name. It is obviously not easy to break free of stereotypes that have for centuries been based on ideas of "nature." Sand's contradictions on the subject, despite the fact that she was able to find words to paint the enslavement of married women and call so forcefully for their civil rights, prove this point and invite further consideration.

Happiness was unfortunately fleeting, and the next two years were particularly trying. For some time Maurice had been showing Manceau thinly disguised hostility. The tension mounted after his wedding and then the birth of his son. Now he was the head of the family and the master of Nohant; at least, that was how he felt. In November 1863 things became even more heated, ugly things were said, so much so that Maurice came out and quite simply demanded that his mother's companion leave Nohant, where he had been living for the last fourteen years. Sand then made an unexpected move, saying she would leave Nohant and go live for a while with Manceau at some place not far from Paris. As Manceau noted in the diary, "I've been told I am free to go by the next Feast of Saint John [June 24]. . . . So I'm going to be free again and if I want to love and devote myself once again, since that is what makes me happy, I'll be able to do so in complete freedom."[199]

Would Sand really leave Nohant? That was hardly imaginable. Sand seems to have dealt with the most pressing matters first, mixing reasons of the heart with practical and financial considerations. It was too expensive to live comfortably in Paris, but it would be good to be near Paris in order to monitor theater rehearsals and performances, including Manceau's.[200] Moreover, it seemed necessary to leave the young couple freer in their movements and to let Maurice manage the property that would one day be his. Finally, Manceau had for some time been suffering from some worrisome symptoms that brought to mind those of Chopin near the end of his life. He kept losing weight, coughed endlessly, and seemed twice his age. In the portrait that Nadar made in 1864, Manceau, his elbow leaning on a thick book on a pedestal table, had the sad look of a worn-out man.

So they separated, but saying they would often be back in Nohant for a couple of weeks. A few months later, in March 1864, Alexandre Manceau bought a "little out-of-the-way house, low down at the far end of town,"[201] with a garden, in Palaiseau, which then had train service to Paris. As Sand explained, "We're going to settle down close to Paris to take care of theater work and other things that will be easier to do here where we are. We've got Nohant on a good footing for the future so that we can be together there for a season every year. This is neither a departure nor an abandonment of the area nor a separation of the family, but an arrangement that makes it easier to live and move about because we also want to do some traveling next year."[202]

In Paris Sand left rue Racine for a modest apartment in rue des Feuillantines, and Manceau worked hard to "clear the place out."[203] Nadar paid her a visit in these "student quarters" and left "heavyhearted," finding the apartment and its Moorish decoration so shabby.[204]

News kept coming from Nohant, and Sand replied by long letters detailing what she was doing, her theatergoing, the success of some playwrights, the "flops" of others, the rehearsals of her own plays. She missed "Cocoton," for whom she would be the godmother at a Protestant baptism. Manceau sent his "regards and best wishes."[205]

Sand started looking at her accounts and her son's: "I think that to stay at Nohant within your budget your expenses must not exceed your income and that Lina's dowry plus Mauricot's work has to pay for the little jaunts and traveling that you want to do, all quite feasible once Cocoton is weaned, meaning next fall."[206] When the works of Eugène Delacroix were put up for sale after his death in 1863, Sand pointed out to her son that "the flower painting will probably fetch a good price":[207] "If you want to sell, *now's the time*. . . . I'd like to hang on to the *Centaure*, for as long as I live. It was his last gift, and the *Confession de Giaour* was his first. There are still the *Saint Anne*, the *Fleurs*, the *Cleopâtre*, 2 *Lélia*, the *Chasse au lion*, the *Carrières*, several sketches, horses, corners of the garden, rough drawings, a watercolor lion, Mickiewicz's portrait, etc."[208]

What marvelous works! Were her financial needs so pressing? Just then Sand was asking lots of people she knew for money and demanding a raise from the director of the *Revue des Deux Mondes*. She convinced the banker Édouard Rodrigues to help her out, and she would sell him *L'éducation de la Vierge*, which Delacroix painted during one of his stays at Nohant. As for Maurice, he decided to sell all the works of Delacroix in his possession, but it was not easy, nor did he realize the expected profits.

In early June 1864 Maurice, Lina, and their son left Nohant for Guillery in order to introduce the young Marc-Antoine to Baron Dudevant. Encouraged by Sand, this move was not altogether without ulterior motives. She was in fact afraid that Casimir would leave his few remaining assets to the daughter he had had with his servant-mistress, which he in fact did the following year, designating the seventeen-year-old Rose Dalias as his "sole beneficiary." She begged Maurice to find an opportunity to clear up this matter with his father, but he had other things to worry about: a few days after their arrival, the baby fell violently ill with dysentery. "*No fruit, no fruit,* for a very long time,"[209] his grandmother promptly advised by letter.

The child grew weaker, with Maurice and Lina watching over him day and night, and everybody's anxiety growing. The telegrams to Palaiseau one day after another do not mention any sign of improvement. Sand wound up taking the train to Agen and racing "breathlessly"[210] to Guillery. She arrived too late on 22 July:

little Marc-Antoine had died the day before, in a final bout of fever. He was buried in the village cemetery. As Sand wrote to Maurice and Lina, "I weep asleep in my bed, out walking, at work, and half the time without a thought in my head, as though I'd become a moron. We have to let nature take its course. . . . But don't let bitterness get the upper hand, my poor children. . . . We will love, we'll suffer, we'll hope and fear, we'll know joy and terror, in a word, we'll go on with our lives, because that's how life is, a terrible mix of things."[211]

In the fall Sand contemplated spending a few weeks at Nohant and talked about money again. She had no intention of burdening the young couple's budget and said as much to Lina:

> Since we can't divvy up our food in the kitchen, for Manceau and me I'll give you an amount of money equal to what you spend on the two of you. No meat for me, but I eat sweet things, which will balance that out. As for Manceau, he certainly doesn't eat more than Mauricot. . . . I'll have Sylvie look after me and help Marie [Caillaud] in the kitchen. I'll pay her on my own, by the day. Then Marie won't have any extra work. I can buy my own candles, but for oil, wood, and coal, I'll contribute half. . . . If I lived on Nohant's income, it would only get smaller, and that's what I don't want.[212]

With Manceau she spent six weeks in Berry, vainly trying to lift people's spirits by writing plays for the little theater. Endeavoring to distract Maurice from his grief, she did not spare his pain while he was trying to write a novel entitled *Raoul de La Châtre*, a medieval fantasy a bit on the bawdy side.[213] This was a second novel for Maurice, who had published *Callirhoé* as a serial in the *Revue des Deux Mondes* in the spring of 1863 and then as a book with Michel Lévy, who also published his mother's novels. Despite good reviews, the novel was rather a flop. After reading and revising the manuscript, then correcting the proofs, Sand was pleased to see the book come out. She promptly asked all the critics she knew to review it: "Give this man whom you knew as a child, who has